Restoring the Vision

RESTORING THE VISION

The Gospel and Modern Culture

Lawrence Osborn

MOWBRAY

Mowbray
A Cassell imprint
Villiers House,
41/47 Strand,
London,
WC2N 5JE

387 Park Avenue South,
New York,
NY 10016-8810

First published 1995

British Library Cataloguing-in-Publication Data
A catalogue record for this book is available from the
British Library.

ISBN 0-264-67330-1

Printed and bound in Great Britain by
Biddles Ltd, Guildford and King's Lynn

Contents

Introduction

This book has grown out of my involvement with The Gospel and Our Culture, a programme initiated by the former British Council of Churches to explore the relationship between contemporary culture and the Christian gospel. The work of the programme led eventually to an international consultation on 'The Gospel as Public Truth' held at Swanwick in July 1992.

At the end of the consultation I was invited to write my personal response to the entire process. The temptation was to prepare a report of the consultation proceedings. However, I was spared that temptation by the sheer complexity of the consultation. Four hundred people met together for a week in eight parallel mini-conferences, each with the freedom to set its own agenda. In addition, those conferences interacted both formally (through a variety of plenary sessions) and informally (during free time). Anyway, such a report would fail to capture what was for many people a most important aspect of the consultation: the worship. Using traditional and modern, liturgical and extempore styles, the worship managed to express a unity in diversity that enabled Christians from many different traditions to praise God together.

The invitation to respond to the consultation has forced me to examine what I understand by the call to relate the good news of Jesus Christ to contemporary culture. A major influence on my own thinking (and, indeed, on the entire Gospel and Our Culture programme) has been the life and work of Bishop Lesslie Newbigin. Anyone familiar with Lesslie's work will recognize his influence upon my summary of modern culture in Part I. His clear and uncompromising overview of the shape of modernity is often ascribed to forty years' missionary experience in India.

However, I believe another factor is at work. We in the West can see the underlying assumptions of our culture more clearly today because many of us are no longer comfortable with them. In Part II, 'Winds of Change', I explore some crises that have nurtured this discomfort, and various alternative ways forward which have been proposed. We stand at a cultural crossroads. It is important, with Lesslie, to take a critical look at the road we have taken to get here. Perhaps it is time to change direction. But, if so, it is no less important to take a long hard look at the routes which would-be guides are eager to offer us.

And how does the Christian gospel relate to all of this? Does it relate at all? In the final section of the book I explore what is meant by 'gospel' and look at various ways in which Christians through the ages have attempted to relate their distinctive message to the assumptions and practices of the surrounding culture. I suggest that the gospel is not the property of the Church. On the contrary, it has the capacity to transform even the least faithful of Christian institutions when its voice is heard. Finally, I explore certain facets of Christian belief and practice that may be increasingly relevant in a culture undergoing some of the changes described in Part II.

CHAPTER 1

The way we do things around here

THE SCOUSE DEFINITION OF CULTURE

According to Derek Worlock, Roman Catholic Archbishop of
Liverpool, the title of this chapter is the Scouse definition of culture.
It is admirably broad and brilliantly simple. But, he admits,

> it led me into difficulties when I duly trotted it out at an
> international conference in Rome . . . For when I was in
> Rome yet again some considerable time afterwards I heard a
> speaker solemnly define culture, allegedly in my very own
> words, as 'the way things are done in Liverpool'. It was not
> well received: put down, I have no doubt, as a further example
> of English arrogance.   (GPT 1992, 39)

CULTURE AND ÉLITISM

A Scouse definition of culture! The idea! Many people would look
upon this as incongruous, if not absurd.

We need not look far for the cause of this reaction. The word
'culture' is popularly used in an élitist way. A cultured person is one
who attends (or listens to) every Promenade Concert except the

Last Night; who regularly goes to the theatre but has never been to an Andrew Lloyd Webber musical; who prefers Radio 3 to Classic FM; who watches Channel 4 if he or she watches television at all; who reads the *Guardian* rather than the *Sun*. Terms like refined, discriminating, sophisticated, elegant, erudite and 'high-brow' come to mind as possible alternatives to 'cultured'.

This élitism carries over into talk of the culture of a society. 'Culture', in its modern usage, has been with us less than two hundred years. It was popularized by the Romantic reaction against the levelling effects of the Enlightenment.

In Germany, *Kultur* came to denote all that was 'not adequately understood through the grid of Enlightenment reason – things about tradition; about religion; about the feel, the spirit, of a people; things that are precious, and which cannot be put into the mincing machine of this kind of rationality' (Newbigin 1991a, 2). For the German Romantics, *Kultur* embodied the spirit of the German people; something that was not amenable to assimilation by the (French) Enlightenment concept of 'civilization'.

In a similar way, Anglo-Saxon Romanticism promoted 'culture' as a response to the mechanistic spirit driving the industrial revolution. The Romantics extended the notion of personal 'cultivation' to society as a whole. Thus, in their hands, 'culture' became a vehicle for expressing the quality of life of society.

Culture, in this sense, is a set of standards by which we can measure the merit of a work of art, the performance of a system of education, etc. As Matthew Arnold put it, 'the great aim of culture [is] the aim of setting ourselves to ascertain what perfection is and to make it prevail' (cited by Montefiore 1992, 2). Thus it is not equally open to all members of society. On the contrary, it is the particular province of an élite: a 'priestly' caste that mediates true culture to the unenlightened masses. But such élitism breeds contempt, as witness Matthew Arnold's dismissive summary of Victorian England: 'Our society distributes itself into Barbarians, Philistines, and Populace', by which he meant the uncultured upper class, uncultured middle class, and uncultured lower class respectively.

The continuing effect of this élitism may be seen in the distinction between 'high' and 'low' or 'pop' culture. The latter is often a term of abuse: 'pop' psychology suggests a treatment of the subject that is accessible to a wide range of people and therefore need not be taken seriously by those 'in the know'. 'High' culture, on the other hand, refers to 'a body of artistic and intellectual work of agreed value and the processes of making and sharing in this work' (Eagleton and

Wicker 1968, 35). This suggests the world of Oxbridge senior common rooms, of *TLS* critics, of private viewings at exclusive galleries.

If culture means a body of work of *agreed* value, one is tempted to ask 'Agreed by whom?' Who sets the standards and how do they use them? Such questions take on particular relevance in the light of contemporary debates about the content of the curriculum in the teaching of English literature. Culture easily becomes a form of social control: if it isn't culture, we are justified in ignoring or even suppressing it. Shakespeare is culture (provided our grasp of Elizabethan English is weak enough to miss the bawdy bits); 'rap' is not culture (because its black creators do not fit comfortably into *our* culture). At times decisions about what is and is not culture have amounted to attempts at cultural genocide. For example, the English waged a long (and unsuccessful) campaign to suppress Afrikaans in South Africa. By denying the accolade 'culture' to certain types of art, music or literature we effectively marginalize those art forms; conversely, by raising something to the status of 'culture', we may make it a part of the establishment, we may tame it.

In view of such considerations, one may feel more sympathetic towards Hanns Johst who, in a quip often attributed to Goering, said 'Whenever I hear the word "culture" . . . I reach for my Browning' (the gun not the poet!).

A BROADER UNDERSTANDING OF CULTURE

However, an alternative descriptive usage has emerged within the last century, largely due to the development of modern sociology and anthropology. A good example of this latter approach is to be found in the 1978 Willowbank Report on Gospel and Culture prepared for the Lausanne Committee for World Evangelization. It asserts that

> Culture is an integrated system of beliefs (about God or reality or ultimate meaning), of values (about what is true, good, beautiful and normative), of customs (how to behave, relate to others, talk, pray, dress, work, play, trade, farm, eat etc.), and of institutions which express these beliefs, values and customs (government, law courts, temples or churches, family, schools, hospitals, factories, shops, unions, clubs, etc.), which

binds a society together and gives it a sense of identity,
dignity, security, and continuity.   (Stott and Coote 1980, 313)

Several general observations may be made about this use of
'culture'.

To begin with, culture in this descriptive sense is not the exclusive
preserve of a creative intellectual élite. On the contrary, it is an
inescapable part of human life.

We all participate in one or more cultures. We all possess (or are
possessed by) beliefs, values and customs. We all share in the life of
cultural institutions. Our lives are moulded by the cultures in which
we live. Conversely, every one of us is involved in shaping our
cultures as we live our lives (even passivity shapes culture by
reinforcing the status quo).

Culture, in this descriptive sense, is a way of talking about all the
ways in which we are human together. Culture refers to things that
are shared with other human beings. Individuals do not create
culture. We create culture together. Again there is a converse. If we
create culture together, it is equally true that culture creates us
socially: it creates group identity. Culture is what distinguishes
Scots from Canadians from Bosnians, etc.

Perhaps most important, culture gives meaning to the world. As
we shall see in the next section, our culture provides us with the
tools we need to make sense of the world around us. Paramount
among them is human use of language.

CULTURE ON THE DISSECTING TABLE

The danger with a broad definition of culture, such as that suggested
above, is that it may be too broad to be useful. If we are to discuss a
culture and subject it to constructive criticism, we must have ways of
identifying and talking about its salient features.

Tools for the job

Christian analyses of culture often fail because they do not
recognize that a range of tools is necessary to do the job.

It is tempting to rely on *the history of ideas* to the exclusion of
other approaches. This is after all the traditional Western way of
approaching culture. There is a strong bias in Western thought
towards the priority of the idea. A creative individual has an idea
that is then expressed in art or literature or technology or politics.

Theory takes priority over practice. The historical development of cultures may then be traced by examining the way ideas and philosophies have emerged, interacted and fallen into disrepute over the centuries.

The weakness in this approach is that it treats most of the culture as secondary to our ideas, theories and philosophies. It assumes a simple causal relation between ideas and culture.

It is simple but untrue. The relationship between ideas and culture is two-way. Fresh ideas may indeed be the occasion for profound changes in a culture. However, cultural changes may also lead to significant changes in thinking. This was first highlighted by Francis Bacon, who pointed to the impact of technological innovation on culture. Thus, for example, the invention of the printing press created the possibility of mass literacy and mass communication. These, in turn, have had major implications for our understanding of human nature and for wider participation in politics. Similarly, the increasing sophistication of clocks has greatly affected the way we in the West order our lives and perceive the world.

The disciplines of *cultural anthropology* and *sociology* provide us with a set of tools that complement the philosophical and historical methods of the history of ideas. However, the distinction between the two disciplines is a subtle one. One recent introduction to sociology suggests that it deals with the social structures of *modern* society (i.e. society as it is affected by Western economics and technology) whereas anthropology 'has the primary task of understanding premodern societies where the economic, social, and political realms are not as distinct as they are in modern societies' (Fraser and Campolo 1992, 56). The distinctions are blurred as we find anthropologists turning their attention to urban and industrial contexts while sociologists discover 'pre-modern' enclaves in 'modern' society.

A recent addition to the armoury of the cultural analyst is *deconstruction*. This may be regarded as a radicalization of the history of ideas in the light of Nietzsche's claim that all truth claims are covert assertions of power. Good examples of this approach would be Michel Foucault's studies of sexuality and madness, in which he seeks to trace the power relationships implicit in these concepts. The affinity with the history of ideas is particularly noticeable in the tendency of deconstructionism to treat culture as 'a series of texts intersecting with other texts, producing more texts' (Harvey 1990, 49).

Symbolic universes

What holds a culture together is a shared way of inhabiting the world. This integrating factor is often called a world-view. According to James Sire, 'A world view is a set of presuppositions (or assumptions) which we hold (consciously or subconsciously) about the basic makeup of our world' (Sire 1977, 17).

When it is couched in these terms, the concept of a world-view is particularly susceptible to an intellectualist interpretation. This is because some Christian cultural analysts regard a presupposition as 'a belief or theory which is assumed before the next step in logic is assumed' (Schaeffer 1968, 177). If this is so, a world-view becomes a set of axioms analogous to the foundations of Euclidean geometry; a series of propositions about reality.

But a common way of inhabiting the world is surely broader than a set of propositions. Consequently, I prefer the term *symbolic universe*. A symbolic universe is a body of largely unexamined fundamental assumptions about our world. These assumptions provide us with 'natural' or 'commonsense' answers to questions about what is really real, the meaning and purpose of the universe, right and wrong, human nature, etc. Thus they play a formative role in shaping our beliefs and behaviour.

It is important to remember that a symbolic universe is 'largely unexamined'. It is *not* a coherently articulated set of propositions. On the contrary, it is largely unconscious. Most of us are probably unable to state our most fundamental assumptions about the world we inhabit.

In fact, a symbolic universe need not be coherent! We may maintain incompatible assumptions about the world. The result is a degree of tension between them. We can live with this, provided it does not become too acute. A good example would be the way in which New Agers (and, indeed, many other members of modern Western society) value both autonomy and interdependence.

Of course, this does not mean that a symbolic universe cannot be articulated. Circumstances may force us to attend to the shape of our symbolic universe. One such circumstance would be exposure to an alien culture. Thus missionaries returning to Britain on furlough may be much more sensitive to our unexamined assumptions than before they first left Britain. Bishop Lesslie Newbigin, whose writings have inspired The Gospel and Our Culture movement, was struck forcibly by the absence of hope in our society as compared with India. A friend who has made her home in the slums of Lima now finds the materialism of British culture extremely disturbing.

Because they are unconscious, the assumptions that make up a symbolic universe are reinforced by deep feeling. A threat to one of these deeply held assumptions is likely to provoke an irrational response. After all, this is the 'natural' way of doing things! Conversely, affirmation of these assumptions is likely to generate a positive response.

The assumptions of a symbolic universe play an integrating role in culture by providing us with the foundations for knowing, feeling and making judgements. A comprehensive symbolic universe may contain assumptions about what is and is not real; the nature of time and space; what we can know; what constitutes a valid argument. Thus it shapes our categories of thought. But it will also contain 'affective' assumptions: assumptions that govern our ideas of beauty, style, taste and pleasure. Thus the clothes we wear, the food we eat, the houses we live in, the art forms that give us pleasure, and even the kinds of people we find attractive may be influenced by our symbolic universe. Furthermore, our symbolic universe may provide us with criteria for deciding truth and falsehood, good and evil; for determining our priorities; for shaping our desires and our allegiances.

Another way in which a symbolic universe integrates culture is through the provision of emotional security. Knowing that others think as we do, dress like us, share our tastes in food and art, creates a sense of belonging.

Finally, a symbolic universe integrates culture by controlling cultural change. An internalized set of assumptions of this kind is a powerful conservative factor. Change is kept within safe limits.

Some readers may wonder how this relates to the notion of a paradigm. In much of the recent literature, 'paradigm' has been used more or less interchangeably with world-view or symbolic universe. However, for the sake of clarity, I prefer to use the term in a more restricted sense. A paradigm is a framework of assumptions that governs the aims, method and content of a particular discipline. Thus it is analogous to a symbolic universe, but more specialized.

Mapping a symbolic universe

As I have already noted, we may map the contours of a symbolic universe by looking at the points of conflict between rival symbolic universes. A complementary approach is to attempt to deduce those contours from the contents of a culture. This latter tactic is analogous to Jung's attempts to map the structures of the psyche from the contents of dreams and myths.

A most important pointer to the shape of a symbolic universe is the language of a culture. Areas of particular richness in a vocabulary often reflect the aspects of reality that are most central to the concerns of a culture. Thus, for example, the Nuer have more than four hundred different words to describe cattle; the various Eskimo languages contain rich vocabularies associated with snow. In North America and Western Europe the multitude of words associated with different consumer goods (e.g. makes of car, types of computer, brands of washing powder) suggest that choice and material consumption are central! Conversely, a lack of words may suggest that the associated ideas are peripheral to the culture, or that it actively represses this dimension of experience. Consider, for example, the relative poverty of the English vocabulary for sexual love.

Another pointer would be the behaviour patterns of the culture. These may be informal: the customs that regulate most day-to-day behaviour. Thus within the sub-culture of Western Christianity there are culturally acceptable reasons for missing church, e.g. sickness in the family, holidays and (in some churches) certain work commitments. But dislike of the new vicar or his style of preaching would *not* be acceptable!

Customs even regulate the culturally permissible forms of suicide: in North America the preferred male technique is to use a gun or a car, the preferred female technique is a drug overdose; in India the preferred male technique is hanging, the preferred female technique is drowning; among Eskimos it is by exposure to the cold.

Other behaviour patterns are formalized into protocols and laws. There are correct forms of behaviour for formal banquets and for acting in the presence of royalty. And there are legal codes that set out a variety of sanctions for those who violate what a culture regards as most important. The tendency of English courts to hand out stiffer penalties for crimes against property than for crimes against the person says something about the values of our culture.

The characteristic artifacts of a culture are yet another indicator of the shape of the underlying symbolic universe. Enormous ancestral(?) stone heads dominated the culture of Easter Island. Today, in the West, the clock is ubiquitous: it is virtually impossible to avoid some analogue or digital indication of the passage of time. What does this say about modern Western preoccupations?

Then there are our symbol systems: myriads of sensory cues that evoke complex responses. The sound of church bells. The smell of carbolic or Marmite. Particular forms of dress indicate how we might be expected to behave towards the wearer: police uniform, dog-collar, mini-skirt and fishnet tights. Again, some of these symbols are formalized, e.g. our complex system of road markings and signs. Finally, words may be used symbolically (e.g. think of the different uses of 'red').

One last area which is helpful is that of myth and ritual. Modern Western culture has few formal rituals, but it certainly does have its myths. By myth I mean a story that enshrines something that the culture regards as a fundamental truth (or truths). Thus it is a story with the potential to bring order and meaning to the world of the hearers. A good modern example is the myth of evolution (as distinct from the biological theory). As a myth it offers us a reason for our existence (a scientific explanation, since our culture puts a premium on this kind of explanation); a coherent cosmology, i.e. it shows us our place in the order of things (in its mythological forms, evolution puts humankind at the pinnacle of a hierarchy of being); a model for social organization (evolution has been used to justify everything from radical socialism to *laissez-faire* liberalism); and an inspirational vision (e.g. the New Age's appropriation of evolution as a spiritual law).

Reinforcing a symbolic universe

Contrary to the prophets of individualism, it is very hard to inhabit a symbolic universe of your own making without reference to others. Human beings are inescapably social creatures, and this, in turn, means that they are cultural creatures. H.G. Wells once wrote a short story in which he questioned the proverb 'In the country of the blind, the one-eyed man is king'. On the contrary, he points out that because the sighted person refuses to conform to the blindness of the culture, *he* is ostracized.

Cultural affirmation makes it much easier to maintain a world-view or symbolic universe. Conversely, if your symbolic universe fails to match that of the culture around you, you will experience tension and conflict. At its most extreme, this produces the phenomenon of culture shock when humans move from one cultural world to another. When this phenomenon is experienced within one's native culture, it is sometimes diagnosed as a form of mental illness. It is debatable whether certain categories of mental illness are genuine medical conditions or forms of social/cultural control.

Sociologists have coined the phrase *plausibility structures* to denote the mechanisms by which the symbolic universe of a culture is maintained, The term refers to 'the processes and social patterns that make given theories and symbolic universes subjectively believable . . . networks of social relationships that enable the people within them to have a strengthened sense that their conclusions are true and right' (Fraser and Campolo 1992, 92).

Plausibility structures include customs and forms of behaviour which are built upon the assumptions of the symbolic universe. As we conform to those practices, our conformity reinforces the underlying assumptions, whether or not we would consciously agree with them. Paul's strictures on the eating of meat sacrificed to idols (1 Cor 8) highlight this point: in certain contexts, the eating of meat could reinforce the symbolic universe of paganism despite the personal religious beliefs of the participants.

Social institutions are another important part of a culture's plausibility structures. Their codes of conduct reinforce the underlying symbolic universe, while their disciplinary powers control departure from the symbolic universe. Thus Ben Johnson is ostracized by world athletics for allegedly taking a banned substance. Deviants may be ostracized, criminalized or hospitalized.

As Os Guinness has pointed out, 'just as the Party is the plausibility structure for Marxism, and the Senior Common Room can be the same for secular humanism, the Church is the plausibility structure for the Christian faith' (Guinness 1983, 36). Like secular plausibility structures, the institutional Church contains practices, mechanisms and networks of relationships which lend plausibility to the Christian gospel. That is why the efforts of certain ecumenical theologians in the 1970s to dispense with the Church were doomed to failure. They failed to recognize the importance of having a social underpinning for any belief system.

A special case of the maintenance and reinforcement of a symbolic universe is the question of how it is communicated to the next generation. The simple answer is that the symbolic universe is 'caught' by participation in the daily life of the culture. That is one function of plausibility structures.

However, in some cultures specialized social institutions have emerged with the specific function of inducting young people into the culture. In pre-modern cultures these are often religious institutions. Ivan Illich, among others, has highlighted this aspect of modern Western education systems. Besides the education system, it is worth noting the emergence of the mass media as a defining feature of Western culture. Indeed, it is arguable that the task of mediating the culture has, to a large extent, now passed from education to the media.

BEWARE OF THE BULL

Christian analyses of culture often suffer from what might be called the 'bull in the china shop' approach. We are tempted to be 'prophetic' in our pronouncements. If we succumb to the temptation, we may end up indulging in unwarranted generalizations about our culture based on inadequate attention to insufficient data.

Thus, in concluding this chapter, I want to issue several warnings to would-be cultural analysts. They also serve as reminders to myself and my readers of the enormity of the task before us, and the inadequacy of any individual to undertake it.

Society is complex

Modern society is not characterized by a single monolithic culture. On the contrary, it is a bewildering complex of sub-cultures and cultural frames.

By *sub-cultures* I mean the many localized cultures maintained by ethnic groups, social classes, young people, etc. By *cultural frames* I mean the variations on public culture maintained by various social institutions. Thus schools, banks and hospitals each have their own particular traditions, customs and codes of conduct.

As inhabitants of such a society, we move freely between several of these loci of culture.

To the extent that a society is a coherent whole, there will be one dominant symbolic universe which determines the relations of all the rest. The Gospel and Our Culture argues that for the past two centuries this role has been played by a symbolic universe which may be named 'modernity'. However, the task of discerning the contours of the dominant symbolic universe is complicated by the plurality of sub-cultures.

Culture is a moving target

Cultures change because the participants change. Some cultures change faster than others. Arguably, modern Western culture changes most rapidly of all as we attempt to cope with a constantly developing technology which gives us access to new possibilities and powers.

Any cultural analysis must recognize the fact of cultural change. However, the available models for understanding cultural change are themselves cultural artifacts (usually closely related to a particular symbolic universe).

Static cultures.   Some cultures have no concept of cultural change. This does not mean that they do not change – history and archaeology suggest that they do. But within such a cultural context change is simply inconceivable. Thus medieval artists depicted biblical events using contemporary architecture and dress.

Cyclical change.   The simplest form of change envisaged by human cultures is a deterministic cycle of growth and decay. It is modelled on our experience of the seasons. Thus, in both Hellenistic and Hindu cultures, change is seen as a never-ending passage through four ages. A golden age of truth and enlightenment gives way gradually to the present age of falsehood and darkness. After an apocalypse, we return to the golden age, and so on.

Gradualism.   This view allows that genuine change occurs. It occurs slowly, by the gradual accretion of new customs and the death of old beliefs and traditions. Cultures are seen as responsive to their environments, gradually adapting to new circumstances. The most familiar forms of gradualism are progressive, namely the various evolutionary myths of Western liberalism. However, gradualism need not be progressive (this is an important point of departure between evolutionism and current evolutionary theory: neo-Darwinism does not regard evolution as progress).

Catastrophism.   According to this view, genuine change comes about dramatically. It is a matter of revolution rather than gradual reform. Again, this has both progressive and non-progressive forms. The best-known type of progressive catastrophism is undoubtedly Marxism. Non-progressive catastrophism is represented by the original (Kuhnian) form of paradigm theory.[1]

An incompleteness theory of cultural analysis

This final note is occasioned by the earlier comment that, as members of a complex society, we move freely between several sub-cultures and cultural frames. However, it is beyond the capacity of any individual to inhabit all the sub-cultures and cultural frames that go to make up our society. Thus there are good grounds for believing that no one can ever be aware of the whole of a culture.

We have no right to presume that we have a neutral, objective (omniscient) perspective on a culture.

Ours is ever only a limited human perspective. It follows that our analysis will always be coloured by our experience. The stockbroker, the MP, the unmarried mother and the unemployed miner will see the culture in different ways. This effect extends even to the way in which we define culture.[2]

Furthermore, the symbolic universe which holds a culture together is pre-conscious. Thus, even if a synoptic overview of culture were possible, we could never be certain that our analysis of it was complete and accurate.

Finally, even if a complete and accurate analysis of culture were possible, it would be out of date by the time that analysis was complete!

Conclusion

This is not a counsel of despair, but rather a plea for humility. What follows is my personal perspective, with all the limitations which that implies. I offer it as a contribution to the continuing discussion about the relationship between the gospel and our culture rather than as a prescription. And I offer it in the hope that elements of it may be helpful in delineating appropriate forms of Christian mission to our culture.

NOTES

1. See Chapter 11.
2. e.g. Niebuhr's famous definition of culture: 'Culture is the "artificial, secondary environment" which man superimposes on the natural. It comprises language, habits, ideas, beliefs, customs, social organizations, inherited artifacts, technical processes, and values' (Niebuhr 1951, 46).

    Looked at from the perspective of the 1990s, two things are striking about this definition. It is an oppositional definition, setting humans over against nature (a clear reflection of the modern Western way of looking at the natural world). And it subsumes woman under man (again reflecting the culture of the time).

PART I

CONTOURS OF MODERNITY

CHAPTER 2

Knowledge is Power

THE BACONIAN VISION

The forces which have shaped the modern world are closely allied to major intellectual movements in Western thought. However, it is an oversimplification to assume that there is a simple causal relationship between ideas and the myriad human practices which go to make up a culture. It is not simply a matter of intellectuals seeking out the wellsprings of the mind in their academic ivory towers and then allowing the results to trickle down to the masses through the influence of their students upon the decision-making of the next generation.

It is grossly unfair to intellectuals to assume that they live in glorious isolation from the problems of the world. Many (probably the majority of) intellectuals feel the troubles of the world deeply. Their debates are not confined to purely abstract matters such as the number of angels that could dance on the head of a pin! On the contrary, a great deal of intellectual activity stems from a deeply felt dissatisfaction with the way the world is. Those who doubt this point should recall that Marx and Engels were intellectuals.

Dissatisfaction with the world as it now is provokes questions such as 'How do I cope?' or 'How can I change it for the better?' Traditionally, answers to those questions have been sought in the spheres of religion and philosophy. Again, those who assume that philosophy is entirely abstract and academic should recall that one of the major philosophical schools of classical Greece was Cynicism: the Cynics focused on practical questions of self-fulfilment and worldly success (the original 'How to win friends and influence people' philosophy).

Herald of a new age

The writings of Francis Bacon (1561–1626) mark a novel departure from that traditional response to dissatisfaction with this present life. Instead of the consolations of philosophy or religion, he proposed that the way to change the world for the better was through technological advance. He was particularly impressed by the ways in which medieval discoveries had already transformed European culture. Thus

It is well to observe the force and virtue and consequence of discoveries, and these are to be seen nowhere more conspicuously than in those three which were unknown to the ancients, and of which the origin, though recent, is obscure and inglorious; namely, printing, gunpowder and the magnet [i.e. compass]. For these three have changed the whole face and state of things throughout the world.
(*Novum Organum*, Book I, Aphor. 129)

In Bacon's view the ills of this fallen world were to be alleviated by the extension of human dominion over nature. But this entails a systematic knowledge of how it works: 'Nature cannot be ordered about, except by obeying her.' Mind you, there was little evidence of such obedience in his recommendation that we put nature to the question (an allusion to the contemporary rack and thumbscrew approach to criminal investigation!).

At a number of points Bacon anticipates subsequent trends. For example, he was the first to use 'fact' in its modern sense as a concept which is divorced from (and opposed to) values, opinions and beliefs. Similarly, his interest in the workings of nature was narrower than that of his predecessors. For Bacon, what mattered was cause rather than purpose. This marks a shift from a personal to an impersonal view of nature. It also gives the technologist *carte blanche* to manipulate the natural world. Thus, in his most famous aphorism, Bacon could comment that 'Knowledge itself is power'.

This is not to suggest that Bacon was an outright radical. Although he anticipated modernity in a number of significant ways, he was still rooted in the old. For example, his thinking was still very much indebted to the Aristotelian philosophy of the Middle Ages. Bacon himself recognized this, calling himself merely a herald of a new era of scientific and technical achievement.

It is perhaps not inappropriate that many people have seen a connection between the Royal Society and Bacon's vision of Solomon's House in *New Atlantis*, both of them being institutions devoted to the study 'of works and creatures of God'. Of the latter Bacon said 'the purpose of our foundation is the knowledge of the causes and motions and inner virtues in nature and the furthest possible extension of the limits of human dominion'. Or as another translation puts it, 'the enlarging of the bounds of human Empire, to the effecting of all things possible'. And here we have yet another anticipation of modernity: *the possible is compulsory*. One is tempted to retort (with apologies to St Paul): 'All things are possible, but not all things are helpful. All things are possible, but not all things build up.'

The Enlightenment project

The European Enlightenment of the seventeenth and eighteenth centuries is usually thought of as an intellectual movement *par excellence*. Thus when commentators trace the roots of modernity to the Enlightenment they are often accused of focusing only on the history of ideas. But, in fact, the Enlightenment was more than just an intellectual movement. Its leading lights were also concerned with social reform.

Specifically, they were concerned with the reconstruction of European culture and society in the wake of the devastating religious wars which were an unforeseen consequence of the Reformation and Counter-Reformation. Those wars had high-lighted the potential divisiveness of public religion. The visible Church was no longer a tenable basis for social unity. The Thirty Years War represented an unravelling of the Constantinian settle-ment which had put the Church at the heart of European politics for more than a millennium.

Faced with the death throes of Christendom, some Christians saw the way forward as depending upon a radical separation of Church and state. Thus the Pietists promoted what might be called the first ecumenical spirituality: an approach to the Christian faith in which personal experience of God's grace supplanted doctrinal correctness. Many leading figures of the German Enlightenment (not least Kant himself) grew up in that context.

But the Enlightenment was far more radical than the Pietist response. Its leaders saw a crying need for an alternative to the Church as a basis for social unity.

Both the need and its solution are epitomized in Descartes' famous *Cogito, ergo sum*, 'I am thinking, therefore I exist'. Descartes was searching for certainty in a world of war, famine and confusion. The experience of reality as decay and impermanence led him to adopt a profound scepticism about the world. Even God was no longer viable as a basis of certainty. Descartes was utterly alone in a hostile environment. Those three words represent a significant paradigm shift. All he had left was his own rational activity. And it was to that he turned as the foundation for certainty: 'I am thinking, therefore I exist.'

It is important to note that he developed his basis for certain knowledge over against external realities. Thus at the very heart of his theory of knowledge there is a dualism between rational activity and all other reality. It should also be noted that the way his search was formulated, as a search for certainty, sharpens the distinction already noticed in Bacon between fact and value, knowledge and belief.

Thus, based on a foundation of reason, the Enlightenment project for social reform was a radicalization of the Baconian vision which David Harvey has summarized in the following terms:

> The idea was to use the accumulation of knowledge generated by many individuals working freely and creatively for the pursuit of human emancipation and the enrichment of daily life. The scientific domination of nature promised freedom from scarcity, want, and the arbitrariness of natural calamity. The development of rational forms of social organization and rational modes of thought promised liberation from the irrationalities of myth, religion, superstition, release from the arbitrary use of power as well as from the dark side of our own human natures. Only through such a project could the universal, eternal, and the immutable qualities of all of humanity be revealed.   (Harvey 1990, 12)

The anti-dogmatic principle

Harvey's summary of the Enlightenment project highlights a feature which is implicit in my description of the background to the Enlightenment. It is what Cardinal Newman called the anti-dogmatic principle.

Implicit in the turn to reason is a sense that the old authorities have failed. They could not prevent the carnage of the Thirty Years War. Thus the angry young men of the Enlightenment raised the banner of reason against the ranks of all the old irrationalities. In the name of reason they opposed myth, dogma, superstition, tradition and external authority.

Of course, also implicit in this attack on forms of knowledge not susceptible to reason is a devaluation of more personal forms of knowledge.

TECHNICAL REASON

Narrowing the scope of reason

Strictly speaking, the Enlightenment turn to reason was not so much a turn from unreason but a concentration on a particular type of reason. Furthermore, as Paul Tillich points out (Tillich 1967, 29–34), it was not the intellectual leaders of the Enlightenment who were responsible for this concentration. Tillich himself distinguishes four types of reason which were still in use during the period we call the Enlightenment: universal reason (recognition of the intelligible ordering of the universe), critical reason ('a full, passionate, revolutionary emphasis on man's essential goodness in the name of the principle of justice' (Tillich 1967, 32)), intuitive reason (descriptive or phenomenological reason), and technical reason.

It is this last type of reason which has come to dominate Western thought since the Enlightenment. Again, Tillich gives a helpful description of it: technical reason 'analyzes reality into its smallest elements, and then construes out of them other things, larger things' (Tillich 1967, 33). Technical reason proceeds by a process of analysis or reduction and synthesis or generalization. A problem is solved by breaking it down into manageable components. Understanding is achieved by reducing a situation to its fundamental components and then describing how those components fit together. This is the kind of reason which gives rise to that knowledge which Bacon could identify with power.

The scientific method

Technical reason reaches its most refined state in the various descriptions of the scientific method (and, above all, of method in the physical sciences). It is sometimes said (usually by physicists) that there are two types of science: physics and stamp-collecting.

The 'stamp-collecting' approach is that associated with Bacon and the empirical tradition in philosophy. Here scientists are content to collect data. They then look for recurring patterns in the data. Those patterns allow them to make certain generalizations. Of course this happens in physics as in other sciences. Thus, for example, Ohm's Law relating potential difference, current and resistance in an electrical circuit is an empirical generalization of this kind.

Classical physics succeeded in refining this process to something like the following:

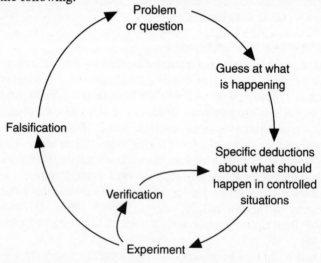

Of course this is an idealization. In the real world, physical science is a less tidy and more exciting process. But most practising physicists would have in the back of their minds some notion of the scientific method which looks not dissimilar to this.

Implications of technical reason

The spectacular success of technical reason, of the scientific method, in providing us with knowledge of reality which we can use to fashion everything from microwave ovens to weapons of mass destruction has led many men and women in the modern world to deify it. We often hear it suggested that science is 'that which has always made us distinctively human', 'that science is or can be the complete and only explanation' (Appleyard 1992, 2). This is the language of the quasi-religious doctrine of scientism: the belief that science can furnish a complete explanation of reality; an explanation, moreover, which holds out the possibility of salvation from all that afflicts us and may ultimately lay bare the mind of God.

Only a minority of practising scientists hold such an exalted view of their subject. However, even when it is not consciously affirmed, there is a widespread tendency to look to scientific or technical reasoning as *the* solution. This exclusive concentration on technical reason has a number of implications for the modern Western mind-set.

Quantification. The demand for specificity in the scientific method combines with Descartes' characterization of matter as extension to produce an emphasis on quantification. 'Now, what I want is, Facts . . . Facts alone are wanted in life' says Mr Gradgrind in Dickens's *Hard Times*. Furthermore, to be taken seriously as scientific facts, they should be measurements.

In early classical physics this was taken to the extreme of classifying the physical features of an object into primary and secondary qualities. Only the primary qualities (which could be measured in metres, seconds and kilograms) were of concern to the physicist. Secondary qualities such as colour, taste and temperature were peripheral (until physicists developed the concepts and techniques required for making measurements of these).

This tendency has extended far beyond physics. In modern economics, only what is measurable in pounds and pence is real. 'Success and failure are measured by statistics; so is amount of work, ability, intelligence and performance' (Stewart 1972, 68). Because they are quantifiable, credit ratings tend to take priority over personal assessments of a client's honesty.

A corollary of this emphasis on measurability is a tendency to believe that bigger is better. Success is measured in terms of the biggest bank balance, the largest number of research publications, the biggest congregation.

Pragmatism. Reliance on experimental verification (or, more accurately, falsification) relates to another notable characteristic of the Western mind-set: our tendency to be pragmatic. Truth is what works, and it is true only so long as it works. In other words we have a problem-solving attitude to the world. What matters is not the truth or the morality of the means, but the fact that it works.

Either–or thinking.   The important deductive element in the scientific method highlights another feature of Western ways of thinking. Most of us operate with a binary logic: yes–no, true–false, right–wrong, practical–impractical, good–bad, legal–illegal, moral–immoral, virtue–sin, success–failure, clean–dirty, civilized–primitive, extrovert–introvert, work–play. One most important example of this tendency to create dichotomies is the public–private dichotomy which will be the subject of a later chapter.

For such a mind-set, neutrality is not acceptable. If you are not for us, you are against us. Consider American reactions to Nicaragua. The Sandinistas were against Somoza, who was for the USA; therefore they must be against America. It was simply not conceivable that somebody might be opposed to one of your allies without necessarily taking a stance against you.

Reductionism.   The sheer power of the analytical approach to reality can be enchanting. It is only too easy to fall into the trap of assuming that analysis into component parts gives a complete explanation of every situation. This is the doctrine of reductionism, or 'nothing buttery'.

But a piecemeal approach to problems can be dangerous in the real world. A 'good' example was the developed world's response to Egypt's energy problems. The obvious answer was hydroelectric power from the Nile. And so the Aswan Dam was constructed. However, this had a number of unforeseen but devastating side-effects. The dam reduced the flow of silt down the Nile, resulting in a loss of fertility in the farm lands bordering the river and a decimation of the fish stocks at the mouth of the river. The dam also produced a large body of standing water, perfect breeding conditions for the bilharzia snail (the carrier of a parasite which causes one of the most serious debilitating diseases of the Third World).

Rational planning.   Combining an emphasis on technical reason with faith in human progress results in a planning-orientated mind-set. We set goals and achieve them, we foresee problems (provided we have not been blinded by our own analysis) and avoid them. We are in control, the masters of our own destiny.

THE RATIONALIZATION OF THE WORLD

The price of success

Neither the founders of modern science nor the fathers of the European Enlightenment focused exclusively on technical reason. They could still see the value of the other forms of reason referred to above. However, the very power of technical reason tempts us to concentrate on it to the exclusion of other forms of reason. Its success in delivering tangible material progress (genuine improvements in hygiene and health care as well as VCRs and Nintendo machines) has permitted a certain idealization, if not idolization, of science and technology.

One effect of this idolization is that the means of attaining knowledge has become a primary criterion for its validity. How often are the terms 'unscientific' or 'irrational' used rhetorically to dismiss the assertions of our opponents? It is true that 'unscientific' can be used in a narrow technical sense merely to denote potentially legitimate forms of knowledge which have been obtained without recourse to the scientific method (or which are not susceptible to empirical testing). But most uses of the word are not of this kind.

Consider the following analogy. If we liken truth to the water in a well, this exclusive concentration on technical reason would be like demanding that the bucket used to collect the water be a certain shape. Water is obtained only from round buckets. The colourless tasteless fluid in that triangular bucket is not authentic water. The absurdity of the position only becomes clear when we take it to such extremes. Thus few people today would maintain the logical positivist position that assertions which are not susceptible to empirical testing are strictly 'non-sense'.

Nevertheless, while we might shrink from taking such a view to extremes, we do as a society place far greater store by 'scientific' knowledge than by knowledge attained in other ways. Even New Agers who assert the superiority of intuition over technical reason are eager to point out that their intuitions are supported by the latest scientific speculations.

Technological optimism

The idolization of technical reason leads naturally to its extrapolation to every conceivable situation. All situations may be formulated as problems. And all problems are, in principle, soluble by recourse to technical reason.

Christianity has often been accused of demystifying the world. There is a degree of truth in this, in the sense that it has desacralized the world. In orthodox Christian theology the world as a whole is put firmly in the category of creature: it may be sacramental, but it is not, in itself, sacred. But the triumph of technical reason takes the process of demystification to the furthest extremes. It denies to God's creation any continuing mystery.

It asserts that everything is laid bare by the right application of technical reason. Of course this does not amount to a declaration of human omniscience (or even potential omniscience). But at the practical level it leads to the widespread assumption that everything can be solved by a suitable technological fix. Even death becomes optional – at least, that is the hope of those wealthy American technological optimists who have had their corpses deep frozen!

Technological optimism is such a deep-seated assumption in Western culture that it is recognized in environmental literature under the technical name 'technocentrism'. This is the establishment response to environmental crises: they are treated as problems susceptible to technological solution. Thus depletion of the ozone layer by commercially produced halocarbons is taken as a challenge to develop new refrigerants which do not have this effect. The result is a proliferation of new technologies in answer to the unforeseen problems of older technologies. But there is little recognition of the likelihood that these new technologies will also have unforeseen environmental consequences. One country's solution to the energy crisis is another country's acid rain!

Rational social organization

Technical reason has given us an unprecedented degree of mastery over the natural world. Technological optimism presents us as the astronauts in control of spaceship earth. But the advocates of technical reason have never been content to restrict it to the realm of non-human nature. One of the characteristics of modernity is the extension of technical reason to the problems of human nature and social organization. Sociologists speak of this as the rationalization of society.

The effects of rationalization can be seen everywhere. They are set in stone (or rather concrete) in the high-rise housing estates of modernist architecture. There was an entire school of architectural thought devoted to rationalizing the way we live. Their goal was to bulldoze the slums and the winding streets, the untidy mixture of housing, commercial property and industry which emerged as the modern city began to evolve in the nineteenth century. In its place they thought to put properly planned apartment blocks in neat rows with the various aspects of daily life reflected in a zoning of the city for maximum efficiency. Thus, in the words of a 1910 edition of *Good Housekeeping*, the house became 'a factory for the production of happiness' or, as Le Corbusier was to put it some years later, a 'machine for modern living' (Harvey 1990, 23).

The rationalization of the world can also be seen in the emergence of one of the major modern schools of psychology, behaviourism. This school of thought restricted psychology to the study and prediction of observable patterns of human behaviour. It rejected explanations in terms of 'mind' on the grounds that they were not susceptible to empirical testing.

Yet another sphere in which the rationalization of life can be seen is in the radical changes in industrial practice which have taken place during the twentieth century. The theory behind these changes can be traced back into the nineteenth century, but it was the opening of Henry Ford's automated car assembly line at Dearborn, Michigan, in 1914 which really marked the beginning of this revolution. With the advent of Fordism in Western working practices came the extensive rationalization of our use of time. The recent introduction of computers into the workplace has greatly extended that rationalization. Now it is possible for employers to monitor the efficiency of office workers electronically (number of seconds per telephone call, number of keystrokes per hour, etc.)

A VERY VISUAL CULTURE

It is often suggested that we are only now moving from a word-based culture to a visual culture. Instead of books, our offices and schools are increasingly dominated by TV screens and WIMP[1] driven computers. But this is a superficial assessment. In fact, books *are* visual. Written words are abstract visual symbols which evoke certain concepts (often they evoke far more than just the plain meaning of the words themselves). Hearing the spoken word is a very different experience from reading the same words. Thus a society which bases its storage and transmission of knowledge on the written word will develop in a different way from one which bases them on the spoken word.

This relates to our emphasis on technical reason, because it was a crucial technological development (a specific application of technical reason) which made this possible. As Francis Bacon pointed out, the printing press wrought a massive transformation of Western culture. It is worth noting in passing that this was not a case of technology being driven by pure science. Rather, it was the application of technical reason in the sense of our rational problem-solving abilities. Technology is often thought of as the application of science but, historically, it is at least as accurate to see science emerging as an abstraction from technology.

Abstraction

Interposing a text between a speaker and hearer has the effect of encouraging abstraction. Reading a book is less personal than listening to a story-teller. The trustworthiness of the source becomes less important than the merit of the ideas themselves. Thus we focus on the ideas and, as a result, tend to build up systems of ideas which are not directly related to everyday experience.

Mass information storage

The book and, more recently, the computer have provided Western culture with an unprecedented capacity for storing information. Again, this lends itself to an abstract systematizing approach to knowledge (perhaps reflected in the shift in emphasis from wisdom, to knowledge, to information).

It is salutary to recall that the origin of writing lay in the need of prehistoric city states to maintain official records. In other words, writing began as a device for social control: 'Anything you say may be taken down and used in evidence against you.' Information storage serves the needs of those who control society. The advent of sophisticated computer databases means that modern governments (and other powerful social institutions) know more about their citizens than ever before. An extreme case is Singapore, which, thanks to its advanced public transport system, has the capacity to monitor the movements of its citizens to an unprecedented degree.

Objectivization

Technical reason and the dominance of visual metaphors for knowing in our culture lead to an emphasis on *objective* knowledge. We know things as detached observers; a tendency which is further reinforced by the dualism inherent in Descartes' approach to knowledge.

This objectivity has given rise to a myth of neutrality: scientific knowledge is reputed to be pure description, free of any value judgements. But, in fact, such objectivity is far from neutral. On the contrary, it is highly selective because the personal dimension has been effectively excluded from the realm of knowledge.

The impersonality of such knowledge has important implications. It takes us out of the realm of personal (I–Thou) relationships into that of impersonal (I–It) relationships. Thus it is the agent of master–slave relationships rather than personal relationships. In our culture a truth claim is implicitly a power claim. Scientific/technical reason is coercive.

RELIGION IN AN AGE OF REASON

The rationalization of the public world does not mean that our culture has abolished the 'irrational'. Far from abolishing it, modernity has allowed the irrational to flourish in private. Thus throughout the period since the Enlightenment there has been a flourishing occult underground, often attracting influential members of society and leaders of culture. Thomas Carlyle, W.B. Yeats, Katherine Mansfield, Rimbaud and Baudelaire were just a handful of those involved in this hidden world.

What the triumph of technical reason did was to erode the *plausibility* of religion. Because religion was not amenable to this one type of reason, it was presented as *ir*rational and consigned to the same outer darkness as astrology and tarot cards.

Faced with such a situation, Christian theologians accommodated themselves in one of two ways. Either they reasserted the rationality of religion or they admitted that religion was not a matter of knowledge.

Religion beyond knowledge

This strategy plays on the incompleteness of technical reason. Anyone other than a logical positivist will admit that there is more to life than the empirically testable. An exclusive reliance on technical reason calls into question the whole area of values, morality and ethics (after all, ethical assertions such as 'murder is wrong' cannot be tested empirically). Similarly it devalues intuition, imagination and creativity. Thus it is possible to conceive of entire domains of human experience which lie outside the scope of science. One can protect religion from science by locating it exclusively in one (or more) of these realms.

Many of the more sophisticated theological responses to the Enlightenment were of this type. Thus Schleiermacher insisted that the basic building-block of theology was religious feeling. Alternatively, Ritschl and his fellows put the emphasis on ethics: 'the fatherhood of God and the brotherhood of man'. Such efforts were extremely successful. But, in fact, their weakness lay in their success: they managed to carve out private niches for themselves beyond the scope of science. By doing so they reinforced the privatization and marginalization of religion which is such a characteristic feature of modernity.

Rational religion

The alternative to admitting the dominance of technical reason was to argue that religion was rational in the same sense that science is rational. This strategy could take either a liberal form (recasting religion within the limits set by technical reason) or a conservative form (refuting the rational arguments against traditional forms of religious belief).

The liberal version restricted religion to what could be shown to be consistent with a scientific understanding of the world. And, given a closed mechanistic understanding of the cosmos, there was no place for God except as the absent watchmaker who set the cosmic machine in motion but has no continuing relationship with it (the religious option known as deism).

The conservative form emerged considerably later than deism and has proved more resilient. Fundamentalists operate with essentially the same impoverished theory of knowledge as their modernist opponents. They simply stand the Enlightenment position on its head, arguing that evolutionary science fails to meet the criteria of technical reason.

NOTE

1. An acronym denoting 'windows, icons, mice and pointers', i.e. the whole gamut of graphical interfaces which have been devised to make computers more 'user-friendly'.

CHAPTER 3

Nature and
Nature's Laws

Nature and Nature's laws lay hid in night;
God said, *Let Newton be!* and all was light.
(Pope)

CARTESIAN DUALISM

Not only did Descartes' solution to the problem of impermanence
lead to the new approaches to thought discussed in the previous
chapter, but it led to new ways of categorizing the world itself.

In Descartes' case, the changes and chances of this fleeting world
reduced him to a state of radical doubt about the reliability of his
senses. It was so radical that no amount of observation could
overcome his scepticism about his own existence. Only the for-him-
indisputable fact of his own rational activity was sufficient assurance
of his own existence. In his *Meditations*, he proceeded from that
basis to prove the existence of God and, thence, of physical reality.

What is significant, in the present context, is the way in which
sense perceptions (and hence empirical knowledge) have been
reduced to the status of mere opinions. On the other hand, the
'clear and self-evident' ideas which are the product of rational
activity are elevated to the status of certain knowledge. This

elevation of reason over the senses very naturally suggests a twofold division of reality. In his own words:

> from the mere fact that I exist, and that I do not observe that any other thing belongs necessarily to my nature or essence except that I am a thinking thing, or a substance whose whole essence consists in thinking. And although perhaps . . . I have a body to which I am very closely united, nevertheless, because, on the one hand, I have a clear and distinct idea of myself in so far as I am only a thinking and unextended thing, and because, on the other hand, I have a distinct idea of the body in so far as it is only a extended thing but which does not think, it is certain that I, that is to say my mind, by which I am what I am, is entirely and truly distinct from my body, and may exist without it.   (Descartes 1968, 156)

Thus Descartes bequeathed to subsequent generations that division of reality into subject and object which has come to be known as Cartesian dualism. In this way of looking at reality, there are two fundamentally different aspects to the world. On the one hand, there is *res cogitans*: the intelligible realm, the province of subjectivity, of mind, soul and spirit (and, hence, of religion and supernature). On the other hand, there is *res extensa*: the material realm, the province of nature and science.

It is important to realize the novelty of this dualistic outlook. Earlier thinkers had certainly been aware of the differences between mind and matter, but they never sharpened those differences into the kind of dualism introduced by Descartes. Rather, they understood mind and matter as opposite ends of a continuum (the Great Chain of Being). As R.G. Collingwood points out, classical thought took it for granted that nature was permeated by mind, 'that mind belongs essentially to the body and lives with it in the closest union' (Collingwood 1945, 6). In fact, the philosopher of science Stephen Toulmin argues that this novelty marked the death of cosmology:

> all the dualisms and dichotomies that have been characteristic of science and philosophy since the year 1600 – separating Humanity from Nature, Mind from Matter, Rationality from Causality, and the rest – were foreign to the thought of antiquity, and became influential only during the modern period. So understood, the world view of Descartes and

Newton no longer represents a genuine *cosmos*. Instead, it is split down the middle; and as Pascal liked to insist when he poked fun at the menial tasks imposed on Descartes' *Dieu philosophique*, it took the continual effort and attention of a benevolent God to prevent the two halves of the new scientific world picture from falling apart and to keep them operating together in harmony. (Toulmin 1982, 224)

In making this sharp distinction between mind and matter, Descartes had clearly articulated a metaphysical perspective which was in the ascendancy. Unlike other aspects of his philosophy (notably his extreme rationalism), this dualism was accepted with little opposition. For example, John Locke is often presented as offering the empiricist counterbalance to Descartes' rationalism. But Locke, like Descartes, works with a dualism of passive sense and active reason (Gunton 1985, 17). Similarly, Kant (who is widely regarded as having effected a reconciliation between rationalism and empiricism) pushes this latter dualism to its logical conclusion with his assertion of the mind's dominion over the material world: 'We must . . . make trial whether we may not have more success in the tasks of metaphysics, if we suppose that objects must conform to our knowledge' (Kant 1933, 22).

THE DETACHED OBSERVER

Descartes' subject–object scheme provided fresh justification for the classical commitment to *theoria*. This can be traced as far back as Aristotle, who first set up the contrast between the activity of the philosopher (*theoria*) and the *praxis* of the carpenter or farmer. Recalling the roots of the word, Toulmin notes that 'the philosopher was thought of as a "spectator" with a touch of class or official status – even with a touch of holiness about him' (Toulmin 1982, 239).

In the light of this ideal, the preferred outlook of the scientist was one of detachment or objectivity. For Descartes, objectivity implied universality: it was a generalizing and quantifying outlook. By contrast, personal knowledge (and any knowledge derived from participation) cannot be generalized in the manner of geometry. It is superficial, unreliable and subjective when compared with the rational, fundamental and geometric knowledge of the virtuoso and *philosophe*.

Buoyed up by the initial optimism of the Age of Reason, the ideal of detachment was epitomized by the Laplacean image of the omniscient calculator. From his quasi-divine perspective, the scientist was, in principle, able to attain a comprehensive and perfectly accurate account of the motions of all particles at all times. To achieve this, all that was required was a knowledge of their initial positions and trajectories, and an accurate account of the laws of physics. There was no uncertainty in this model.

THE WORLD AS OBJECT

Bacon and Descartes provided the infant science of Western Europe with an extremely powerful technique, namely concentration upon the world as an object. Detachment from the world enabled the scientist to avoid those philosophical difficulties which have come to be known as the paradoxes of self-reference. In general, we find it much more difficult to articulate an explanation of those phenomena in which we participate than of those of which we are merely spectators. Consider the poor centipede in the poem who was able to walk until asked for an explanation of how she co-ordinated all her legs!

Furthermore, regarding the world as an object, rather than a living organism of which we are an integral part, gives the scientist and technologist *carte blanche* to predict and control. It entails an I–it (or master–slave) relationship with the material world rather than a personal relationship.

But what kind of world was this Cartesian *res extensa*? According to Descartes, matter is entirely passive (as opposed to mind/spirit, which is active). Thus it is entirely receptive to the mathematical laws imposed upon it by God. It follows that matter must be quantifiable: it must have geometric extension (Kaiser 1991, 163). However, its very passivity precludes it having any innate qualities beyond those associated with extension. Thus, for Descartes, the material world was a world without forces and, hence, without causal relationships. 'There was only a continuum of material bodies in relative motion sustained by the continual re-creation of God' (Kaiser 1991, 163).

A similar understanding of the material world was already to be found in the writings of Galileo. He categorized the properties of matter into primary and secondary qualities. The latter, including taste, sound, smell, colour and temperature, he dismissed as subjective. The former, namely mass and velocity, were objective properties of matter independent of the observer and, hence, alone worthy of the attention of the physicist. Descartes' material world was a world reduced to Galileo's primary qualities. It was a world of mere extension, devoid of anything which would excite the interest of anyone other than the physicist.

MECHANISM AND CAUSALITY

Descartes' conception of the physical world was clearly inadequate even by the standards of physicists who were his contemporaries. In particular, the notion that the material world was devoid of forces and causality created serious difficulties. It reduced the physicist to recording recurring coincidences. Moreover, it committed Cartesians to a doctrine of occasionalism: in simple terms, an understanding of the world as a sequence of static creations of God. In such a universe there would be no change, only the illusion of change. Cinema offers a good analogy: what you see on the screen is the illusion of change created by running a sequence of static images through the projector.

In view of these inadequacies, it was not long before the Cartesian world-view was supplemented. By introducing the concept of force, it was possible to move beyond the Cartesian world of particles in motion to the Newtonian one of law-abiding mechanism.

The world machine

The picture of the world as a great machine has fascinated people since the seventeenth century. It was to become one of the mainstays of natural theology, with the design of biological structures (such as the human eye) being likened to the design of complex human artifacts. In spite of some reversals, the machine metaphor is still with us today. Our machines have simply become more sophisticated. Today we find physical scientists likening the universe to a vast computer, or even to a programme running on some non-physical transcendent 'hardware'.

However, the machine metaphor has a number of striking implications for the way we look at the world around us.

Descartes had already applied the machine metaphor to the animal kingdom. He rejected the concept of animal souls on two grounds: that even the higher animals showed no signs of intelligence, and that animal immortality was absurd (Williams 1978, 282–3, 287). Thus the motions of animals could not be distinguished from other purely physical motions. That which we interpret as animal 'behaviour' is merely the result of a physical disturbance in the animal's nervous system. It is an unconscious reflex. Thus the mouse's reaction to a cat (or, for that matter, the cat's reaction to the mouse) is an automatic response, behaviour caused mechanically by certain stimuli.

In denying consciousness to animals, Descartes was denying them purposes of their own. But advocates of the world machine have gone far beyond this. They have deduced from the machine metaphor that there are *no* purposes immanent in the physical world. It is true that a machine is created for a purpose, but that purpose is external to the machine itself. In the case of creation, its purpose is knowable only by divine revelation. Thus it seemed perfectly proper for Christian mechanicists to support the methodological exclusion of purpose from the physical sciences.

A deterministic cosmos

With the exclusion of purpose, physical scientists turned their attention to efficient causality, i.e. to the physical factors which brought about a particular event or state. In a mechanistic cosmos there are only particles in motion, exposed to physical forces of various kinds. The events within the purview of the physicist are essentially changes in uniform motion. These are caused by forces (either contact forces, i.e. collisions, or action-at-a-distance, e.g. gravity or magnetism).

It is only a small step from saying that physics is only concerned with efficient causes to saying that all events may be completely explained in terms of those same efficient causes. Thus classical physics moved smoothly and rapidly into determinism typified by the outlook of Laplace.

A deterministic view of the material world is quite consistent with the Cartesian insistence on the passivity of matter. Agency, and hence freedom, is the exclusive prerogative of conscious souls. Matter moves, but without purposes of its own. The physical world is in the thrall of the laws of physics (and, one might add, the free agency of immortal souls).

The world as a human resource

This emphasis on the passivity of matter and the corresponding reduction of all non-human life to the level of 'natural automata' (Descartes cited by Williams 1978, 282) offered an easy justification for the increasing exploitation of the natural world as the industrial revolution got under way.

Such a world has no innate purpose, meaning or value. In the wake of Kant, it was natural to suppose that any value or purpose in creation was the result of the observing mind's conceptual creativity. It followed that it was perfectly proper for the natural world to be treated as raw material to be utilized by humankind.

The pervasiveness of this outlook and its inherent incapacity to respond constructively to the contemporary environmental crisis are highlighted by Oliver O'Donovan when he comments:

> Thus arises the irony of our own days, in which the very
> protection of nature has to be argued in terms of man's
> 'interest' in preserving his 'environment'. Such a philosophy
> offers no stable protection against the exploitation of nature
> by man, since he can discern nothing in the relations of things
> to command his respect.   (O'Donovan 1986, 52)

Mechanism and society

This mechanistic outlook on the world is reflected in and reinforced by the extensive mechanization and bureaucratization of Western society. I have already commented on this to some extent in the previous chapter. Suffice it to say that the rationalization of which I spoke there is tantamount to an assertion of the mechanistic model: rationalizing a factory assembly line is essentially an exercise in making the machine operate more efficiently.

Factories and bureaucracies are two very effective ways in which our culture passes on its mechanistic outlook to the next generation and to the rest of the world. In terms of its output, the modern factory says very clearly that the material world is *raw* material to be moulded to our purposes. More subtly, the assembly line, the division of labour, specialization and standardization all have the effect of extending the machine analogy to the work force. Bureaucracies with their standardization of human roles have a similar effect. Today we are all cogs in a machine.

NATURE'S GOD

The triumph of efficient causality meant that every event was explicable in terms of preceding events. Thus the natural world came to be seen as a self-sustaining mechanism.

The concept of specific divine action is very hard to reconcile with such a world-view. One option (the one adopted by conservative

Christians) was to see divine action in interventionist terms. If the world is a self-sustaining machine, specific acts of God can only be seen as the acts of a *deus ex machina* who operates by means of miracles. And, of course, miracles have to be redefined as violations of the laws of nature. But clearly such a God violates the integrity of that which he has created; such a God is coercive.

However, there is one loose end left in this otherwise seamless robe of efficient causality. The mechanistic cosmos can sustain itself, *given* an initial ensemble of particles in motion. There is still room in the mechanistic world-view for a God who is its First Cause. Thus,

> The first Almighty Cause
> Acts not by partial but by gen'ral laws.
> (Pope 1733, 1.145–6)

The result is the watchmaker deity of deism: an artisan God who assembles the world machine and sets it in motion. Such a God is entirely external to the world. What is more, any subsequent divine actions (adjustments of the mechanism) are liable to be taken as evidence of the imperfection of both creation and creator. If God really is omniscient and omnipotent, goes the argument, he should not need to tinker. Such a God is to all practical purposes irrelevant.

In fact, the Enlightenment view of God is more complicated than this thumbnail sketch of deism would suggest. Alongside the absolute transcendence of deism we find ample evidence for the persistence of a pantheistic (or panentheistic) view of God.[1]

This latter option arises out of considerations of the extent of the material universe. Descartes had been content to leave this indefinite, but other thinkers[2] insisted that extension had to be infinite. This has serious theological implications (Koyré 1957, 152–3). If, following Descartes, extension and matter are identical, it implies that the material universe is infinite and therefore divine: God is excluded. The alternative adopted by More (and subsequently by Newton) was to distinguish matter from extension or space. Thus we have a finite material cosmos embedded in an infinite space. The latter (together with time) is raised to the status of an attribute of God (Kaiser 1991, 179). Thus we find Newton describing God in the following terms:

> a powerful ever-living Agent, who being in all places, is more able by his will to move the bodies within his boundless

uniform sensorium [space], and thereby to form and reform
the parts of the Universe, than we are by our will to move the
parts of our own bodies.   (Newton cited by Kaiser 1991, 182)

As this quotation suggests, the analogy for divine action which
recommended itself to Newton was that of the relationship between
mind and body. Pope, as ever, puts it more sharply:

> All are but parts of one stupendous whole,
> Whose body Nature is, and God the soul.
> (Pope 1733, 1.267–8)

Thus, in addition to the deistic outlook, we find the panentheistic
conception of the world as God's body creeping into the literature
of the period.

NOTES

1. Pantheism is the belief that the universe itself is God. Panentheism holds that the
   universe is contained within God (e.g. that the world is, in some sense, God's
   body), but that it does not express the fullness of God.
2. For example, Henry More, one of the Cambridge Platonists, and Newton's
   mentor.

CHAPTER 4

Time, History and Progress

THE IMPORTANCE OF TIME

The ubiquity of time

Time travels in divers paces with divers persons. I'll tell you who Time ambles withal, who Time trots withal, who Time gallops withal, and who he stands still withal.

. . . Who ambles Time withal?

With a priest that lacks Latin, and a rich man that hath not the gout; for the one sleeps easily because he cannot study, and the other lives merrily because he feels no pain, the one lacking the burden of lean and wasteful learning, the other knowing no burden of heavy tedious penury. These Time ambles withal.

. . . Who stays it still withal?

With lawyers in the vacation; for they sleep between term and term, and then they perceive not how Time moves.

(Shakespeare, *As You Like It*, 3.2.329–55)

As Shakespeare's Rosalind points out, our experience of the passage of time is highly subjective. It is proverbial that the rate at which it passes changes with age: time apparently passes more slowly for children. The passage of time is also affected by our hopes and fears. The seconds seem to tick away more rapidly when we anticipate something unpleasant. They slow to a crawl when something pleasant approaches. At times we may even cease to be aware of time's passage altogether.

But whatever our experience of time, it is an inescapable feature of human life. It characterizes every aspect of our lives: our work, our leisure and our relationships all unfold within time. Time is the medium in which we live our lives.

Because time is so fundamental, the attitude we adopt to it will have far-reaching effects. It will leave its mark upon everything we are and do. According to the theologian Robert Banks, 'If our attitude [to time] is flawed, then all that we are and hope to become, along with everyone and everything we touch, will be flawed also' (Banks 1983, 11).

This applies as much to our cultures as to our individual lives. For example, the theologian Robert Jenson has suggested that the fundamental difference between Roman Catholicism and Protestantism is the issue of being in time: Catholicism understands this in terms of institution whereas Protestantism understands it in terms of freedom (Jenson 1992, 107).

Telling our stories

Because of its ubiquity, our attitude to time is bound to have an impact on our self-understanding, both individually and communally. It will affect how we tell our stories.

If time is understood as a meaningless cycle of birth and death (or primarily as the medium of death, decay and defection), such negativity will rub off on the way we tell our stories. A negative attitude to time will encourage ahistorical forms of story-telling. We will communicate our self-understanding through myth and ritual rather than through history. The implications of this are very far-reaching. Such a denial of time tends to encourage a type of mysticism which insulates the mystic from contingent human experience and, hence, from personal relationships with others. Commenting on the contemporary Western revival of paganism, the sociologist Carl Raschke maintains that 'In the endeavor to stop time, man runs the risk of undercutting his relations with others; indeed, he threatens to stab to death his very humanity' (Raschke 1980, 22). In a similar vein, Tillich accuses paganism, with its emphasis on space and corresponding denial of time, of being inherently unjust (Tillich 1964, 38).

Alternatively, if time is understood as having meaning and a direction, we are more likely to express our self-understanding in the temporal form of history. This is more then a mere recording of bare historical facts. In fact, those works which do claim to be mere chronicles of the historical facts are often implicitly selective. For example, the chronological passages of the Old Testament, far from being mere chronicles, convey an implicit theological message. Similarly, the *Anglo-Saxon Chronicles* were written as much to legitimate contemporary political power structures as to record what had happened in the past. History always involves a process of interpretation. The decision to report that William of Normandy defeated King Harold at the Battle of Hastings is based on interpretative criteria about what is and what is not significant. As Eric Ives points out, 'Intervention and interpretation by the historian is a necessary and integral part of the study of history. What happened, happened – the past itself is an objective absolute – but that is not true of the way we know it' (Ives 1992, 17).

The providential view of history

Just as in science there are no uninterpreted data, so in history there are no uninterpreted historical facts. Thus when we produce a history we will invariably base it upon certain selection criteria which may be explicit or implicit. There are certain things which we will regard as significant and others which we will pass over as unimportant. As feminists point out with a good deal of justification, the fact that the recording of history has been a male preserve in Western culture means that specifically female experiences have been passed over as irrelevant. Our selection criteria will reflect the culture in which we have been brought up, but they will also affect it, as our reading of history through these spectacles will influence the next generation.

The most fundamental interpretative framework for history in the West for over a thousand years, from the time of Augustine to the demise of Christendom, was what has been called the providential view of history. David Bebbington summarizes it as follows:

Christians . . . have normally adhered to . . . three convictions about history: that God intervenes in it; that he guides it in a straight line; and that he will bring it to the conclusion that he has planned. The three beliefs together form the core of the Christian doctrine of providence.   (Bebbington 1979, 43)

Thus history was organized on the basis that God was in charge of historical events. Strictly speaking, Bebbington is wrong to describe this as intervention. As I pointed out in the previous chapter, it is only in the past couple of centuries that people have come to think of God's providential care for creation in terms of intervention in an autonomous order. Augustine's view (which became the consensus in classical Western theology) was that God acts *through* all creaturely events:

> In his providence God does not 'work' in history as one external cause among other causes (though for the tradition he may well so work in miracles), but always in and through the various dynamic factors, including freedom, effective in all historical change. (Gilkey 1976, 161)

But there was more to the providential view of history than that God acts though historical events. Above all, it was the conviction that time was directional and orientated towards God's ultimate goal. Again, we might question Bebbington's way of expressing this: time was directional, but not necessarily 'a straight line'. A more appropriate metaphor for pre-industrial Western approaches to time would be that of a stream: it has a direction, but its flow is variable; it is not rigidly quantitative; the engineers have not yet turned it into a canal; it is not yet clock time.

THE MYTH OF PROGRESS

The demise of providence

The decline in the providential understanding of history coincided with the collapse of Christendom because of the radical changes in our understanding of the world and of human nature which were then introduced.

One important factor in the demise of providence was the emergence of the mechanistic world-view described in the previous chapter. According to one commentator, 'The Cartesian mechanical theory of the world and the doctrine of invariable law, carried to a logical conclusion, excluded the doctrine of Providence' (Bury 1920, 73). The reason for this was simply that, if every event can be adequately explained in terms of finite efficient causes (i.e. causal factors *within* the world), divine action too became subject to natural law. This clearly places severe limits on the scope of divine action.

Broadly speaking, if we accept the mechanistic world-view, we are forced to interpret divine action in one of four ways. The most conservative option is *interventionism*: this retains a more or less orthodox view of God but limits his involvement in the world to isolated miracles (now understood as violations of the laws of nature). More consistent (and extremely popular during the heyday of the Enlightenment) was *deism*: the view that a truly omnipotent God would not need to tinker with the perfect mechanism of his creation at all. A third possibility favoured by some theologians was *omnicausality*, i.e. that *all* events are caused by God (this reflected the older view of providence but distorted it by denying creaturely freedom). Finally, there was the option of *pantheism*, which effectively identified God with the natural order.

Another factor in the demise of providence was the Enlightenment's 'turn to the subject', its emphasis on human autonomy. This will be explored in greater detail in the next chapter. Suffice it to say that, in relation to history, this emphasis on human autonomy implied that history was the product of human rather than divine activity (Gilkey 1976, 243).

The idea of progress

The pantheistic tendency of Enlightenment thought may be seen in the way in which attributes of God were transferred to the natural world. This process is clear in the transition from faith in divine providence to faith in progress. The first stage was the increasing mechanization of providence: it was increasingly treated as a natural law-like phenomenon. From here it was but a small step from regarding it as an attribute or activity of God to treating it as an immanent law of nature. Thus emerged what Tillich has called the Enlightenment principle of harmony: the hidden hand governing the functioning of the market and generally ensuring that, whatever the motivations of individuals, the overall tendency of human society is in the direction of ever greater harmony.

Progress was regarded as an inevitable law of nature. Thus Herbert Spencer could write: 'progress . . . is not an accident, but a necessity . . . . what we call evil and immorality must disappear. It is certain that man must become perfect' (cited by Bebbington 1979, 85).

Affinities between providence and progress are not hard to find. True, an immanent natural principle has supplanted a transcendent God. But otherwise progress is very similar to its predecessor. The directionality of time becomes increasingly linear and quantitative, as befits a view of time intended for a mechanistic world. Instead of the divine purpose, the direction of history is now determined by the limitless improvement of the human lot. Thus we find statements like

> I profess no belief in the perfectibility of man or in a future paradise on earth . . . But I shall be content with the possibility of unlimited progress – or progress subject to no limits that we can or need envisage – towards goals which can be defined only as we advance towards them, and the validity of which can be verified only in the process of attaining them. (E.H. Carr cited by Ives 1992, 27)

Given these affinities, it is hardly surprising to find that people readily identified divine providence and human progress. Thus, for example, Lord Acton insisted that 'Not to believe in Progress is to question the divine government' (cited by Ives 1992, 27). From a very different perspective, Simone Weil could argue that 'Primitive Christianity concocted the poison represented by the notion of progress' (Weil 1956, 615).

However, in spite of these affinities, providence and progress are entirely incompatible. Indeed, it would not be an exaggeration to describe progress as the antithesis of providence. One of the crucial functions of the doctrine of providence (at least as it was formulated by Calvin) was to counter a fatalistic outlook. By shifting from the personal care of an active deity to inexorability, progress reintroduces fatalism, albeit with a smile on its face!

The tangibility of progress

In spite of the barbarities of our own century, faith in the inevitable and indefinite improvement of human society remains strong. Thus the historian E.H. Plumb could declare:

> It is to me the one truth of history – that the condition of mankind has improved, materially, alas, more than morally, but nevertheless both have improved. Progress has come by fits and starts; retrogressions are common. Man's success has derived from his application of reason, whether this has been to technical or social questions. (cited by Ives 1992, 29)

This quotation introduces another important feature of the idea of progress. One of its strengths is its adherents' insistence on its tangibility. Human progress can be measured. There are rational criteria by which we can judge that progress has occurred. This is, of course, in sharp contrast with the older providential view in which disasters and retrogressions might themselves be an integral part of God's purposes.

These rational criteria take their simplest (one is tempted to say 'crudest') form in the world of economics. The measurability of progress implies that it can be quantified. Material progress is easily quantified by translating it into monetary terms. Thus progress is identified with economic growth. On a public level this has led to our modern obsession with ever-increasing gross national products. Similarly, on an individual level we find the emergence in the West of an acquisitive lifestyle which equates ever-increasing possessions with success.

Progress as a cosmological myth

But progress is much more than a principle of historical interpretation. Precisely because it shapes our histories, it is a principle of self-understanding: it enables us to make sense of our place in human history and in the cosmos as a whole. It retains some of the religious significance of the Christian doctrine of providence.

Thus progress captured the eighteenth-century imagination. The whole of reality was interpreted in progressive terms as a dynamic reality gradually moving towards perfection. Thus, one eighteenth-century author could write 'All creatures from the worm to the seraph must be capable of perfecting themselves' (Lenz cited by Lovejoy 1936, 251). This idea that the whole of nature was creatively advancing itself towards perfection was widespread among writers of the time. An eloquent example comes from the pen of Leibniz:

> A cumulative increase of the beauty and universal perfection
> of the works of God, a perpetual and unrestricted progress of
> the universe as a whole must be recognized, such that it
> advances to a higher state of cultivation, just as a great part of
> our earth is already subject to cultivation and will hereafter be
> so more and more . . . there will always, on account of the
> infinite divisibility of the continuum, remain over in the abyss
> of things parts hitherto dormant, to be aroused and raised to a
> greater and higher condition and, so to say, to a better
> cultivation. And for this reason progress will never come to an
> end.   (cited by Lovejoy 1936, 257)

The dynamism engendered by the idea of progress had a tremendous impact on eighteenth- and ninteenth-century thinking about the natural world. It was in this context that evolutionary ideas came to the fore. By the time Darwin published his *Origin of Species*, evolutionary speculation had been rife for generations. Indeed Darwin's own grandfather, Erasmus Darwin, had written an epic poem embodying evolutionary ideas. Biologists are quick to point out that Darwin provided them with a mechanism for diversification and speciation and that there is no implication that some species are 'more evolved' than others. However, so entrenched was the doctrine of progress by that time that it was inevitable that people would infer from Darwinism scientific support for progress.

Contempt for the past

A further feature of modern attitudes to time which, in part, relates to faith in progress is a tendency to be contemptuous of the past.

Right at the outset of the modern era it was asserted as a fundamental principle that necessary truths of reason could not be derived from history. This principle, popularly known as Lessing's Ditch, effectively set up a stop sign to warn people against seeking truth in history. Since Christianity had hitherto based itself upon a historical revelation, that was one of the first casualties. The notion that 'history is bunk' is one that continues to be reasserted on rational grounds.

But faith in progress would be likely to result in contempt for the past quite apart from this problem of historical knowledge. The reality of progress implies that the future will be better than the present. It follows that the past must be inferior to the present. This was reflected in the seventeenth-century battle of the ancients and the moderns: until that time classical scholarship was treated as superior to modern scholarship. But changing attitudes enabled scholars to shake off the shackles which bound them to Plato and Aristotle. Faith in progress managed to suppress this prejudice in favour of the past and created an atmosphere in which change might mean improvement rather than decay.

However, a further shift in our thinking and behaviour has taken place. We now often behave as if change entails improvement. Change has become an idol of Western culture. Cosmetic alterations to motor cars and consumer goods are hailed as major innovations. So important is change for the modern world that it has

found its way into definitions of modernity. According to Baudelaire, 'Modernity is the transient, the fleeting, the contingent'. Even
John Henry Newman (who was in important respects anti-modern)
could say 'Here below to live is to change, and to be perfect is to
have changed often'.

Implicit in this idolization of change and devaluation of history is
a lack of respect for pre-modern social orders. It has translated into
a dismissal of pre-modern cultures which, in turn, legitimated the
aggressive cultural imperialism which has characterized Europe and
North America in the nineteenth and twentieth centuries. In the
nineteenth century we talked about civilizing the heathen; today we
talk about developing the underdeveloped world. Perhaps the
greatest 'success' of this process has been to educate the leaders of
those 'underdeveloped' countries to perceive themselves and their
peoples through Western eyes.

There is a still more sinister side to this contempt for the pre-
modern. In addition to legitimating cultural imperialism, it has been
used very effectively to legitimate racism. We see this to some
extent in the reception accorded to Herbert Spencer's social
Darwinism. But it appears most clearly in the theosophical
spiritualization of progress with its belief that from the Aryan race
would emerge a spiritually superior 'sixth race' to carry forward the
spiritual evolution of humankind. While mainline theosophy never
overtly preached racism, some of its offshoots provided spiritual
sustenance for proto-Nazism.

THE TYRANNY OF THE CLOCK

Studs Terkel records the following comments from a former airline
reservations clerk about the impact of the computer:

> You were allowed no more than three minutes on the
> telephone. You had twenty seconds, 'busy-out' time it was
> called, to put the information in. Then you had to be available
> for another phone call. It was almost like a production line.
> We adjusted to the machine. The casualness, the informality
> that had been there previously were no longer there. They
> monitored you and listened to your conversations. If you were
> a minute late for work it went on your file. You took thirty
> minutes for lunch, not thirty-one! If you got a break you took
> ten minutes, not eleven! I was on eight tranquillisers a day.

With the airline I had no free will. I was just part of that
stupid computer.   (cited by Banks 1983, 22–3)

That may be an extreme example, but most of us will, at one time
or another, have had the experience that there are simply not
enough hours in the day. This, too, is characteristic of our
experience of time in modernity.

The mechanization of time

One of the factors which, I argued, led to the demise of providence
was the emergence of the mechanistic world-view. But this
mechanization of the world suggests a corresponding mechanization of our metaphors for time.

I suggested earlier that for pre-modern Westerners the directionality of time might have been likened to that of a stream: a stream is
natural and flexible. In the words of Shakespeare, 'Time travels in
divers paces with divers persons'.

Under the impact of mechanization, different metaphors become
dominant. Time moves in a straight line. It is measured by
machines: indeed clocks become a metaphor for the world mechanism, e.g. Robert Boyle's description of the universe as 'a rare clock
such as may be that at Strasbourg'. How do we speak of time under
such a regime? We speak of 'the unforgiving minute'.

The rationalization of society

Another factor in the modern sense that time is oppressive is the
rationalization (or mechanization) of society, on which I commented earlier.

It is sometimes argued that our sense of the oppressiveness of
time is partly a result of technological advances in the measurement
of time. Proponents of this view seem to be very impressed by the
quantum leap in the accuracy of chronometers over the past few
centuries.

However, I would suggest that far more important has been the
changing social role of the clock. At one time the clock was closely
associated with the church tower. In other words, it was associated
with the regulation of a daily pattern of worship. Elsewhere its
primary role was that of status symbol rather than regulator.

Later the clock found its way into the workplace. The requirements of efficient mass production required that workers be
educated in a new attitude to time. Flexible working hours could no
longer be tolerated. Clocks were introduced into the workplace to

regulate and co-ordinate the activities of large numbers of people. This development has today reached its logical conclusion. It would probably be more accurate to speak of the tyranny of a mechanized (and consequently depersonalized) society than of the tyranny of the clock.

CHAPTER 5

Life, Liberty
and Happiness

> We hold these truths to be self-evident, that all men are
> created equal, that they are endowed by their Creator with
> certain unalienable rights, that among these are life, liberty
> and the pursuit of happiness.

The American Declaration of Independence sounds a note which
has become a recurring feature of the modern world. Words like
liberty and equality are so commonplace that we take them for
granted. However, these words have a distinctly modern meaning.

WHAT IS ENLIGHTENMENT?

As I have already pointed out, the Enlightenment was not primarily
a movement of speculative philosophy. On the contrary, it was
highly critical of what it regarded as the unwarranted speculations
of earlier metaphysics. Immanuel Kant, whose later philosophy
represents the high-water mark of the Enlightenment, devoted
much of his philosophical labours to the effort to bring metaphysics
under rational control.

   The movers and shakers of the Enlightenment were driven by
their dissatisfaction with Western society. Years of religious strife
had left them with the conviction that Christendom was no longer a

viable option. The fundamental question underlying all their philosophical deliberations was an ethical one: how can we create a better society?

Dare to know

In a famous essay explaining the term Enlightenment, Kant referred his readers back to the Roman poet Horace: *sapere aude!* Dare to understand! Dare to know! Or, as Kant himself interpreted it, 'Have courage to use your own understanding!' (Kant 1970, 54).

In other words, for Kant and his contemporaries, the free exercise of human reason was the key to the creation of a more humane society. Implicit in this appeal to human reason is an optimism about human nature which is in striking contrast to the Church's doctrine of original sin. In effect it was a direct contradiction of Christ's assertion that what makes us unclean comes from within.

For modernity, evil is something clearly external to the individual. Thus the defenders of modernity do not look for evil within human beings. Rather, they focus upon social conditions and human ignorance. Human beings act in evil ways because they are oppressed or because they do not know the right. But ignorance too is seen as something external: it is not culpable; it is simply another form of oppression. Thus education becomes an important tool for liberation and social reform.

The ideal of autonomy

But rational knowledge alone is not the whole of Enlightenment. Equally important is that little word 'dare'. Kant calls upon us to *dare* to use our reason, to be bold. The enlightened man or woman is one who has shaken off the guardianship of others. Kant is clear that this requires an act of will, an act of courage:

> Laziness and cowardice are the reasons why such a large
> proportion of men, even when nature has long emancipated
> them from alien guidance . . . nevertheless gladly remain
> immature for life. For the same reasons, it is all too easy for
> others to set themselves up as their guardians. It is so
> convenient to be immature! If I have a book to have
> understanding in place of me, a spiritual adviser to have a

conscience for me, a doctor to judge my diet for me, and so
on, I need not make any efforts at all. I need not think, so
long as I can pay; others will soon enough take the tiresome
job over for me. (Kant 1970, 54)

Thus the key to Enlightenment, the secret of a humane society, is
autonomy. Kant and his fellows advocated that, in order to achieve
enlightenment, we must become laws unto ourselves. That phrase
has strong negative connotations. But, contrary to popular mis-
understandings, autonomy (literally, being a law unto oneself) does
not imply a state of lawlessness. The autonomous individual is not
an outlaw, but one who relies upon his or her own reason to
determine right and wrong. Autonomy is the courage to act in
accordance with the light of your own reason, regardless of
irrational impulses and desires or of the unreasonable demands of
external authority.

Some theologians have been tempted to dismiss autonomy as
wilful rebellion against God. But this is not necessarily the case. As
Paul Tillich points out, many Enlightenment philosophers actually
identified autonomy with the divine will. Thus 'In autonomy one
follows the natural law of God implanted in our own being' (Tillich
1967, 26–7). In other words, it may be interpreted as the state
described by Paul in his letter to the Romans:

when Gentiles, who do not have the law, do by nature things
required by the law, they are a law for themselves, even
though they do not have the law, since they show that the
requirements of the law are written on their hearts, their
consciences also bearing witness, and their thoughts now
accusing, now even defending them. (Rom 2.14–15)

AUTONOMY AND FREEDOM

In popular usage autonomy and freedom are often confused.
However, it should be clear from what has been said above that they
are not identical. Autonomy has a positive content which is lacking
in the modern view of freedom. On the other hand, autonomy and
freedom in the modern sense are closely related. In the essay cited
above, Kant goes on to say 'For enlightenment of this kind [i.e.
autonomy] all that is needed is freedom. And the freedom in
question is the most innocuous form of all – freedom to make public
use of one's reason in all matters' (Kant 1970, 55). In other words,

freedom is the formal condition for the possibility of autonomy.

Freedom in modernity

The word freedom is widely used and the concept is highly valued in our culture. But what do we mean by freedom today? A bird is free; a prisoner is not. In a democratic society we have free elections, meaning that there are no physical constraints on our choice. It seems that freedom is essentially freedom from constraint.

Such a view of freedom is strikingly lacking in content. Freedom is presented as a fundamental value of Western culture. But to say that I am free is to say remarkably little.

Of course none of us is completely free. Our freedom is necessarily limited by the freedom of others. This brings in another fundamental assumption of modernity: the assumption of *equality*. In a society of free individuals there must be conventions for determining how one person's freedom is balanced against another's. For modernity, that convention is equality: money, intelligence, social status, race, sex, religious belief, etc., should all be irrelevant to questions of one's freedom from constraint.

But such a view of freedom represents a significant shift in emphasis from earlier understandings. Prior to the Enlightenment, freedom was essentially relational. One's freedom was dependent upon one's place in the family, in the community, in the wider society. Above all, it depended upon one's relationship with God: freedom was essentially the willing of God's will. Thus freedom was something that was exercised within a network of constraints imposed by one's place in the cosmos, and the acceptance of those constraints was seen as a part of one's freedom.

In modernity the balance has shifted away from constraint. Constraints are seen as a necessary evil, to be minimized as far as possible, provided that does not impair the smooth functioning of society. Thus John Stuart Mill could say that 'restraint *qua* restraint is evil'. In other words there is in the modern view of freedom a tendency to deny (or at least underplay) the obligations imposed by one's relationships.

Such freedom from constraint does have a 'positive' corollary. If I am not constrained to act in certain ways by my relationship with the other, it follows that I am free to manipulate or dominate the other in accordance with my will. Nowhere has this corollary of the modern view of freedom been more starkly realized than in Western society's relationship with the natural world.

From duties to rights

The shift in emphasis which has taken place in our understanding of freedom is illustrated very clearly by the corresponding shift in emphasis from duties to rights. Of course rights and duties cannot be easily disentangled: that I possess certain rights entails that I owe corresponding duties. However, there has been a striking change in the priority given to the two concepts.

The older relational approach encouraged an emphasis on the duties arising from one's place in the community. Thus the slave owed certain duties to his or her master. But the slave-owner also had obligations towards his or her slaves. Indeed, towards the end of the Roman Empire there was a definite trend for people to sell themselves into slavery because, from a certain perspective, the obligations of the slave were less onerous than the civic duties of the master!

While not denying that duties and obligations exist, the modern non-relational approach to freedom has concentrated instead on human rights such as life, liberty and the pursuit of happiness. In other words, it focuses not on the duties I owe to others but on what is owed to me by virtue of my status as a human being.

This naturally begs the question, whose duty is it to ensure the provision of my rights? One plausible answer is the state/society. In the ideology of modern democracy, it is the function of the state to guarantee the freedom of its citizens. It is but a small step to the assertion that it ought also to make active provision for our basic human rights: the safety net of a welfare state.

A more individualistic alternative would be to admit that a claim of rights is a claim against myself. Claiming those rights of another could be seen as a move towards dependence rather than autonomy. Seen in these terms, an assertion of my right to adequate housing is tantamount to seeing the acquisition of adequate housing as a moral imperative justifying the actions that I take to satisfy it. The result is the law of the market (or the jungle).

In its most extreme form, the individualistic understanding of human rights has resulted in the New Age ethic of total responsibility (and its more sophisticated Nietzschean counterpart in the will to power). According to this approach, I am totally responsible for the reality I experience. Such an approach rules out a defence of 'I was only following orders'. Total responsibility implies that the lowly concentration camp guard was a co-creator of the system which killed six million Jews. On the other hand, it also implies that the victims of oppression, illness or violence are responsible for their own suffering.

Individualism

Non-relational views of freedom go hand in hand with individualism. By playing down the claims of society, they elevate the status of the individual relative to the community. The same is true of the concept of autonomy. As Kant defined it, autonomy is highly individualistic: the agent of enlightenment is the autonomous individual.

Thus the individual is perceived to be prior to society. For many people in our culture, society is a fiction. Communal existence is seen in terms of voluntary associations of individuals or of contractual groups. The community is regarded as no more than the sum of its parts.

Because of this emphasis on the individual, members of our culture tend not to seek their personal identity through membership of the group. Of course there are exceptions to this generalization, e.g. some of the youth sub-cultures. But, in a culture which stresses individualism and equality, the quest for identity becomes the quest for personal achievement. This is perhaps clearer in the United States than in Britain, since a mythology of equality is much stronger in the former. As a result, self-assertion and competitiveness are a widespread feature of contemporary Western culture.

Also related to the pressure for individual achievement as a way of creating personal identity is the Western emphasis on private ownership of material goods. A variety of distinctively Western assumptions are in play here. As we have seen, there is a tendency in the West to identify the real with the tangible, the measurable, the quantifiable. Thus achievements which are tangible will be accorded higher status than, e.g. achievements of character. High income and conspicuous possessions rather than moral integrity or simplicity of lifestyle will be regarded as marks of success.

A middle-class perspective

It would be an oversimplification to say that Enlightenment thought was somehow the cause of the attitudes which we have been describing. The relationship between ideas and human behaviour is not a straightforward causal relationship. It is certainly arguable that the intellectual sea-change of the Enlightenment was the product rather than the cause of major social upheavals. I have already noted the political crisis occasioned by the demise of Christendom as one of those factors.

Another factor which might be highlighted is the changing nature of commerce and the beginnings of the industrial revolution. The rise of capitalism brought with it important social changes, not least of which was the emergence of the middle classes.

The Enlightenment was not a purely intellectual movement. Rather, it was an intellectual response to eighteenth-century culture from a particular perspective. Judging by the assumptions and values which have been highlighted so far, it is clear that the perspective was that of the newly emergent middle class. Thus, in his assessment of the Enlightenment, Tillich could conclude that 'Socially it was a bourgeois revolution' (Tillich 1967, 27).

THE CULTURE OF ECONOMISM

Given what was said above about personal success being defined in terms of material prosperity, the third inalienable right listed in the American Declaration of Independence points us to the place of the economy in our culture. It would not be an exaggeration to describe the economy as the chief instrument in modernity's pursuit of happiness.

Economics and modernity

Like many other concepts in use today, economics pre-dates the modern era but has been transformed by the emergence of modernity. Its roots in the Greek, *oikonomia* (literally 'law of the household'), suggest that it has to do with the harmonious functioning of the community. This was echoed in the older use of the term 'political economy' as a branch of ethics.

The impact of modernity upon economics had the effect of remodelling it as a science. Specifically, the methodological assumptions of classical physics were transplanted into the economic field to create the neo-classical economics which dominates modern economic thought (Collier 1992, 105).

Like classical physics, modern economics deals only with what is quantifiable. Thus, for example, the economic definition of welfare is the maximal use of available resources. The effects of such reliance on quantifiability are clearly reductive. This is particularly clear in the area of cost-benefit analysis, where monetary values are assigned to the pros and cons of a project in order to determine its advisability. But, for example, in assessing the costs of a new bypass, how do you assign a monetary value to a breeding ground for rare birds?

Modern economics is also mechanistic in the sense that it portrays the world as a giant machine. Or perhaps the analogy of a classical gas would be more appropriate. In classical physics, a gas consists of myriads of atoms in random motion. It is not possible to predict the individual motions but, by making certain assumptions about the behaviour of atoms, it is possible to predict the overall behaviour of the gas. Similarly in economics, markets depend on the 'random' decisions of myriads of economic agents. However, it is asserted that their decisions combine to create order and harmony.

This emphasis on the 'scientific' nature of modern economics results in the cultivation of objectivity and impersonality, both of which are assumed to be characteristics of classical physics. The impersonality of the world of economics is highlighted by what Karl Marx called the fetishism of commodities. He pointed out that members of pre-modern cultures depend directly on those they know personally: they are aware of the joys and sorrows of the producers. By contrast, modernity, with its dependence upon money and commodities, has effectively depersonalized (and sanitized) the processes of production and consumption. David Harvey notes that 'The conditions of labour and life, the sense of joy, anger, or frustration that lie behind the production of commodities, the states of mind of the producers, are all hidden to us as we exchange one object (money) for another (the commodity)' (Harvey 1990, 101). Thus we are blinded to any injustices which might have occurred in the manufacturing process. For example, how many of us are aware of the appalling conditions of service imposed upon many of the part-time workers who assemble the 'Made in Britain' Christmas decorations that we happily buy from High Street shops in order to celebrate the birth of the One who said 'Blessed are the poor'?

More generally, modern economics reflects the Enlightenment ideal of autonomy. This is perhaps clearest in the assumption of private rationality, i.e. economics is based on the assumption that market decisions are the free rational decisions of individuals. As a corollary, economics also reflects the prevailing individualism. In fact, economists speak of a 'methodological individualism'. In other words, modern economics 'maintains that the facts of the world can only be explained in terms of facts about individuals' (Collier 1992, 113). Furthermore, it assumes that those individuals will be motivated by self-interest. Thus it reflects the competitiveness of Western culture.

However, because of the importance of the market in contemporary Western culture, it does more than merely reflect Enlightenment assumptions and values. It is, in fact, a major medium for the propagation of those assumptions and values. In addition to the points already made, it is worth noting some of the values that are propagated by our dependence upon a market economy. With its emphasis on quantifiability, it is our economic perspective which lies behind the modern understanding of happiness as the satisfaction of tangible wants.

Economics also affects our understanding of justice. The Enlightenment insistence on the equality of human beings could under different circumstances lead to a socialist outlook with an emphasis on distributive justice, i.e. ensuring that goods are distributed according to need. However, under the impact of an individualistic market economy, equality is interpreted as equality of opportunity and justice is seen as commutative. In other words, in our culture a just distribution of wealth would be based not on our needs but upon the merit we gain by our work and effort. Thus Jesus' parable of the vineyard workers (Matt 20.1–13) strikes modern ears as offensive because it implies that God does not reward according to our effort but according to his grace.

Finally, it is worth noting that the very importance of the market in Western thought results in a legitimation of the market mechanism. In other words, the selfishness and conflict which drive the market come to be seen as virtuous.

Economism

The above comments would be significant enough if the market economy was only one in a number of competing paradigms. However, it is arguable that it has become the dominant paradigm of Western culture (Collier 1992, 103).

It is notable that Western social structures are primarily economic. We divide our lives between the supermarket and the office or factory or stock exchange or dole queue. Those of us who work in service industries or government are not excepted, as economic criteria also dominate these spheres. Even in the privacy of our own homes, we allow ourselves to be entertained by media which are shaped by commercial considerations. I am not suggesting that this is necessarily wrong. My point is rather that it is by no means universal: it is a peculiar feature of our culture. Economic life certainly went on in the Palestine of Jesus' day – but it did not dominate society in the same way.

The market economy has been found to be a powerful 'evangelistic' tool for Western culture. Throughout the non-Western world, Western development aid has resulted in the effective suppression of local cultures by Western structures. Today in Romania it is easier to buy a glass of Coca-Cola than it is to buy a glass of the local wine! Kentucky Fried Chicken and Americanized pizzas are on the menu worldwide. Even the phrase 'developing world' bears witness to this cultural imperialism: they are developing in the sense that they are becoming more like us.

The power of the market over our lives is seen in the tendency to regard criticism of the market as subversive. Thus Milton Friedman asserts that

> Few trends could so thoroughly undermine the very
> foundations of our free society as the acceptance by corporate
> officials of a social responsibility other than to make as much
> money for their stockholders as possible. This is a
> fundamentally subversive doctrine.   (cited by Walsh 1992, 13)

Clearly the suggestion that making money is not the be-all and end-all of social responsibility has touched a raw nerve!

Another aspect of the power of the market is the tendency of economic language to penetrate into other areas of human experience. Thus one British educationist notes that today

> Schools are run by managers and the managed, not by heads
> and staff. Universities as well as schools have been known to
> spend a great deal of money on creating a 'corporate image'.
> Schools have 'products' although there is some confusion as to
> whether this is the stuff which is taught or the pupils or
> students who emerge at the end. Everything, especially
> examination results, is now 'audited' even by 'task forces' set
> up to do the job. The whole linguistic apparatus is designed, it
> would seem, to do one thing, to ensure that schools provide
> the socio-economic units necessary for the advancement of
> consumerism.   (Priestly 1992, 3)

Jeremy Seabrook takes this a stage further by noting the penetration of economic language even into our ways of talking about personal relationships:

Do we not now talk of emotional investments, of the returns we get for our relationships? A psychic economics helps us judge whether other people are going to pay dividends, whether a friendship is profitless or rewarding, whether there is anything in it for us or whether it will cost us dear. Relationships become transactions; we shop around, or are in the market for a new affair or perhaps a long-term relationship, or even a one-night stand. Although our stock may be low, as long as we retain the assets of our looks or our brains, we can make capital out of them. We may get meagre returns for friendship, but on the other hand, there is always the unexpected bonus, the pay-off. The bottom line has invaded the recesses of our personal lives, and we all have our price.   (Seabrook 1990, 12)

The market economy is clearly much more for Western culture than a convenient instrument. Its pervasiveness, its resistance to criticism, the extension of its language all point to its great psychological and spiritual significance for modern men and women.

Thus it is arguable that the market economy 'has become the object of a quasi-religious cult' (Seabrook 1990, 11). Writing from a Christian perspective, the economist Jane Collier adds that

Precisely because the culture of economism is a quasi-religion, with a pretence of encompassing the totality of life and of bringing happiness and fulfilment, we find ourselves obliged from a Christian point of view to denounce it as a dehumanizing idolatry, which worships profit made by the strong at the expense of the weak, and is deaf to the word of a God who hears the cries of the poor.   (Collier 1992, 122)

Consumerism

That quasi-religious status becomes even clearer when we look at the associated phenomenon of consumerism. The right-wing American thinker Francis Fukuyama cites 'the ineluctable spread of consumerist Western culture' (Fukuyama 1989, 3) as evidence of the victory of Western liberal democracy.

Notice the way Fukuyama qualifies 'Western culture' as 'consumerist'. Consumerism has become a key characteristic of our culture. Arguably, it is now fundamental to Western self-definition.

Consumerism was already implicit in the nineteenth- and early twentieth-century rationalization of industrial production. Mass production entailed mass consumption in order to be economically viable. This in turn required the re-education of the masses: their buying habits had to be modified to fit the products which were flooding the market.

Driven by this commercial imperative, the advertising industry and modern mass media have succeeded in giving birth to consumerism. This is nothing less than a *cult* of material acquisitiveness. One is tempted to suggest that it has its own cathedrals (supermarkets, hypermarkets and shopping malls), its own priesthood (advertisers and salesmen) and its own means of grace (money). What is quite clear is that, thanks to the dominance of the market economy in Western culture, many of us seek our meaning and identity in material possessions. One might say that the Cartesian dictum *cogito, ergo sum* has become *emo, ergo sum*, 'I buy, therefore I am' – or, as one wit put it, 'Tesco, ergo sum'!

CHAPTER **6**

The Two Worlds of
Modernity

THE TWO WORLDS OF IMMANUEL KANT

Kant's essay *What Is Enlightenment?*, introduced in the last chapter, may be regarded as a manifesto for 'an age of Enlightenment'. In addition to its clear explanation of the meaning of autonomy, it anticipates in a remarkable way one of the characteristic features of modernity.

As I have already noted, modern usage tends to equate autonomy with freedom. Furthermore, we tend to define freedom in negative, formal terms as absence of external interference. The ideal of freedom in modern culture is an absence of limits determining our actions. Only those limits which are necessary for the sake of justice and national security (i.e. for the continued existence and smooth running of human society) are to be tolerated. Such a view of freedom became particularly clear under Thatcherism: in the worlds of industry and commerce the good of maximal freedom was to be achieved by minimal legislation. The slogan 'self-regulation' could almost be a modern dictionary definition of autonomy.

However, freedom does not apply equally across every sphere of modern life. Returning to Kant's manifesto, we discover that when he spoke of freedom he had something quite specific (and limited) in mind. Perhaps for pragmatic reasons[1] he was prepared to accept quite severe limits upon human autonomy: enlightenment depends upon freedom, but only 'the most harmless freedom of all', namely 'freedom to make public use of one's reason in all matters' (Kant 1970, 55).

This may sound to modern ears like a considerable degree of freedom. However, Kant adds that 'by the public use of one's own reason I mean that use which anyone may make of it as a man of learning addressing the entire reading public. What I term the private use of reason is that which a person may make of it in a particular civil post or office with which he is entrusted' (Kant 1970, 55). For Kant, enlightenment requires only the freedom to put scholarly arguments before the reading public. He goes on to make it quite clear that this freedom does *not* extend to the freedom to question or criticize specific decisions, policies or orders of those in authority over us:

> Thus it would be very harmful if an officer receiving an order from his superiors were to quibble openly, while on duty, about the appropriateness or usefulness of the order in question. He must simply obey . . . The citizen cannot refuse to pay the taxes imposed upon him; presumptuous criticisms of such taxes, where someone is called upon to pay them, may be pursued as an outrage which could lead to insubordination . . . In the same way, a clergyman is bound to instruct his pupils and his congregation in accordance with the doctrines of the church he serves, for he was employed by it on that condition.
>
> (Kant 1970, 56)[2]

In the process of setting out these limits, Kant has effectively divided life into public and private spheres. Granted that what we today mean by public and private is almost the reverse of Kant's use, this division is still with us. Indeed it is arguable that it is a dominant feature of modern culture. It is to this feature that we now turn.

THE RETREAT INTO PRIVACY

Privatization

Long before the word 'privatization' was taken over by economists to designate the removal of industries and activities from state control, it was in use among sociologists to describe one of the characteristic social changes of the modern era. Os Guinness defines it as 'the process by which modernisation produces a cleavage between the public and the private spheres of life and focuses the private sphere as the special area for the expression of individual freedom and fulfilment' (Guinness 1983, 76).

This is a social process rather than an intellectual development. The relationship between what has happened in nineteenth- and twentieth-century Western societies and the history of ideas is complex and indirect. It would be false to suggest that Kant's dichotomy between public and private (or Descartes' dichotomy between material and spiritual) was somehow 'the cause' of subsequent social developments. However, it would be equally false to deny that there is a connection or to dismiss the ideas as a mere rationalization of existing social developments.

The situation we are faced with in modernity is that for nearly two centuries there has been in existence an accelerating tendency to withdraw personally from the public world into the security of a carefully circumscribed personal sphere: 'An Englishman's home is his castle' with the drawbridge firmly up! At the same time there has been a less marked but nevertheless real tendency among the middle class (the dominant class of the era) to separate public role and personal identity.

Adjusting to new structures

This process of privatization may be understood as a process of adjustment to new social structures. Some authors suggest that it is a response to nineteenth-century urbanization (e.g. Keifert 1992, 16). However, probably more important were the dramatic changes in the shape of public life brought about by the industrial revolution, the rise of mechanicism and the dominance of rationalism. As I have noted in earlier chapters, public life was increasingly rationalized and mechanized during this period.

Migrants seeking work in the new industrial centres of nineteenth-century Europe and North America were faced with the problem of anonymity. They had been uprooted from a variety of traditional cultures in which their social roles and personal identities would have been clearly defined and symbolized by characteristic types of dress, etc. Such symbols allowed social interaction to take place without the need for excessive personal disclosure. Now they found themselves in an entirely new situation where the symbols of their former roles and identities were meaningless. A similar loss of culture is visible today in, e.g., the slums of Lima: a steady stream of

Quechua Indians swells the population, and on arrival they invariably abandon all the trappings of their indigenous culture.

According to the social psychologist Richard Sennett, such urban-industrial anonymity generates anxiety about the involuntary disclosure of character (Keifert 1992, 17). How do you define your own identity and personal relationships when you are surrounded by an anonymous mass of humanity? Lacking the traditional clues which enabled social intercourse, you tend to adopt the role of observer. You watch those around you for inadvertent clues to their real character: slips of the tongue, clues of dress or behaviour. The stranger becomes the object of your scrutiny. But such behaviour will also create a sensitivity to being observed: while you are watching others for involuntary disclosures of character, they are most certainly watching you for the same.

Strategic withdrawal

According to Patrick Keifert, 'If the stranger's character will be involuntarily revealed, then so will mine. If I locate myself among strangers, I need a safe place from which I can watch and wait. I also need to develop a style of speech and dress that hides from any unknowns who I am' (Keifert 1992, 17).

In short, faced with the threatening attitude of those around me in the public arena, faced with this reduction to an impersonal object of scrutiny, I will make a strategic withdrawal into a secure private space in which I can be myself, express my feelings, let my hair down, without fear of ridicule or shame.

Such an attitude also acts as an effective motive for the development of public styles of dress and speech which effectively suppress individuality. The suit and the bowler hat of the traditional city gent and today's ubiquitous jeans and T-shirts are, in their different ways, uniforms: we dress to conform, to blend in with those around us. Similarly, there are powerful social and psychological forces which encourage us to conform to those around us in style and even content of speech. Thus, in the modern world, it has become extremely impolite to discuss personal matters except under carefully defined conditions. It would be regarded as 'unprofessional' for a doctor to give a patient spiritual advice. This might well be seen as an unwarranted invasion of personal privacy.

Yet another effect of this withdrawal into personal privacy is a shift from participation to passivity. For example, in Shakespeare's day the 'audience' expected to be fully involved in a play: it took place in the round, members of the audience felt free to interact in various ways both with each other and with the cast. Contrast this with the Victorian social conventions which still surround attendance at a 'serious' play or concert: the theatre has become a public place, the players are set apart from the audience, the auditorium is darkened to discourage social interaction within the audience. There are certain exceptions, but they serve to prove the rule.

Pantomime as theatre for children is not subject to the same conventions. Children have not been fully initiated into the public–private dichotomy; they are creatures of the private sphere, and pantomime respects that.

Then there are those comedians and cabaret artists who violate the passivity of the audience, forcing individuals to become participants. The embarrassment of the victims and the uneasy amusement of the audience bear eloquent witness to the power of this convention.

This may be a trivial example, but it serves to illustrate a powerful factor in the way modern society functions. As a result of this withdrawal into privacy we become the passive audience not merely of theatrical productions but, more seriously, of the things that happen around us. We see a black boy being beaten up by skinheads and we look the other way. We hear a girl crying for help and we shut our ears. We see a down-and-out lying in his own vomit and urine and we walk past on the other side. We are just the audience. We are the silent majority.

ONE CIVILIZATION, MANY CULTURES

The city of reason

As I have already pointed out, the Enlightenment was not merely an abstract philosophical movement. It was, more importantly, a movement for social justice based upon a clear vision of the new Jerusalem. In place of Augustine's City of God the Fathers of the Enlightenment put a City of Reason. They looked forward to a future in which humankind would be enabled to achieve its full potential by a universal rational social order.

As we have already seen, this vision was only too consistent with a progressive/evolutionary view of the cosmos. Progressivism implied that the modern world was better than all pre-modern societies. It lent the Enlightenment an evangelistic zeal which all too easily became cultural imperialism.

In defence of culture

As I noted in Chapter 1, the very concept of culture emerged as a reaction against the evangelists of the Enlightenment. Romanticism rejected its levelling effects, specifically opposing the reductionism of the scientific method, the egalitarianism of Enlightenment political thought and the literalistic rationalism which members of the Romantic movement believed to be anti-creative and anti-spiritual. In Germany the Romantic reaction was given additional impetus by the perception that the claims of the Enlightenment had become the tools of French imperialism.

Out of this reaction was born the related concepts of *Kultur* and *Volksgeist*. Instead of a universally valid rational social order, *Volksgeist* denoted the unique genius of a people, an irreducible spirituality which enabled one to say 'He is German; she is French; they are Croatian'. Furthermore, in its earlier forms this was not an evolutionary concept.[3] On the contrary, it implied that all cultures were unique and equally valid ways of being human.

This reaction against the Enlightenment vision of a monolithic rational civilization has had a profound effect upon twentieth-century cultures. Many of the anti-utopian visions of modern speculative fiction are explicit rejections of Enlightenment civilization.

Far from promoting a monolithic global civilization, such an outlook tends towards cultural relativism. Belief in the uniqueness and validity of particular cultures lies behind every nationalism of the past two centuries. Scottish nationalism no less less than Kurdish or Serbian nationalism makes sense only if I believe that there is something uniquely valuable about being Scottish or Kurdish or Serbian.

These relativizing tendencies have been greatly reinforced in our own century by the emergence of multi-ethnic societies. In the West we have had to come to terms with the fact that our cities are no longer dominated by white Europeans. Relativism is one strategy for peaceful coexistence in such circumstances.

The result is a state of tension within modernity. On the one hand, there is still that vision of *one* global civilization. On the other hand, there are the competing claims of a bewildering variety of human cultures.

The role of the two worlds

The New Age movement is a convenient bellwether because of its apparent ability to exaggerate many aspects of modernity. This is certainly true of the tension between global civilization and the uniqueness of local cultures. Leading figures in the New Age movement prophesy the coming of a global civilization through effective computer networking. At the same time they indulge in a highly eclectic and uncritical trawl of human cultures for spiritual insights. How do they manage to reconcile both factors; how do they keep together the one and the many?

The answer is that for New Agers, as for modernity in general, the dichotomy between the public and the private spheres is a powerful tool for resolving the tension. We may hold together the multiplicity of human cultures and the vision of a global civilization by relegating the former to the private sphere. Thus cultural and epistemological relativism rule in private. However, as soon as we enter the public arena we are confronted with a public ideology based upon some variation of the Enlightenment's social programme.

The American dream

Nowhere is this clearer than in the United States of America. The USA is a federal society: many semi-autonomous states held together in a federal unity. However, it is also a federal culture (or federation of cultures).

The misnamed 'melting pot' of America has brought together many different cultures: English, Irish, Scottish, French, German, Jewish, Russian, Ukrainian, Greek, Italian, Hispanic, African-American, Egyptian, Chinese, Vietnamese, etc. But far from melting down into some cosmopolitan hybrid culture, they have by and large remained more or less distinct.[4] They live separately in monocultural urban and suburban ghettos (Chinatown, Little Italy) or intentionally separatist rural communities (such as the Amish communities of Pennsylvania). They retain their own languages (Yiddish, Cajun, Pennsylvania Dutch); their own customs (St Patrick's Day, Burns Night and Hanukkah are probably celebrated with greater gusto in Manhattan than in Dublin, Edinburgh or Jerusalem!); and their own social structures (e.g. the Mafia reflects in urban America the feudal social structures of pre-modern Sicily).

And yet they are *all* Americans! They retain their distinctive cultural identities. But those identities have been privatized, relativized and subordinated to the public ideology of America: an

Enlightenment civilization based upon their equal rights to life, liberty and the pursuit of happiness.

FACTS AND VALUES

The fact–value dichotomy

The evident success of technical reason has had the effect of promoting a dualism in our knowledge. So pervasive is this dualism in Western thinking that it is widely assumed to be commonsense. Thus

> It is one of the key features of our culture . . . that we make a sharp distinction between a world of what we call 'values' and a world of what we call 'facts.' In the former world we are pluralists; values are a matter of personal choice. In the latter we are not; facts are facts, whether you like them or not.
>
> (Newbigin 1989, 7)

In a similar vein Keifert argues that 'The distinction between what is and what ought to be, between fact and value, is at the heart of the modern dogma' (Keifert 1992, 32). Most people simply assume that you cannot get from an 'is' to an 'ought'; that it is not legitimate to attempt to generate a moral imperative from a fact of nature.[5]

Public facts and private values

As the above quotation from Lesslie Newbigin suggests, the dichotomy between facts and values is closely related to the sociological dichotomy between public and private.

The public sphere is held to be the sphere of facts: scientific facts and economic facts. It is the sphere of objective knowledge: knowledge that is propositional and subject to scientific scrutiny. Such knowledge is, in principle, falsifiable by scientific experiment. Thus it is held to be rational knowledge. As Newbigin points out, 'Only what can stand up under the critical examination of the modern scientific method can be taught as fact, as public truth: the rest is dogma' (Newbigin 1989, 5).

Everything that fails to meet the criteria of scientific truth takes refuge in the private sphere. Thus this is the realm of values, or moral imperatives, of opinions, of tastes. Whereas knowledge in the public sphere is held to be objective truth, knowledge in the private realm is regarded as subjective belief. Strictly speaking, this is the realm of the non-propositional and the unfalsifiable. By contemporary standards, it is thus the realm of the non-rational.

Acceptance of this dichotomy has had an impact on our understanding of religion no less than on other aspects of Western culture. It is reflected in the division between fundamentalism and liberalism:

> There are on the one hand those who seek to identify God's revelation as a series of objectively true propositions, propositions which are simply to be accepted by those who wish to be Christians. And on the other hand there are those who see the essence of Christianity in an inward spiritual experience, personal to each believer, and who see the Christian doctrines as formulated during church history as symbolic representations of these essentially inward and private experiences.   (Newbigin 1989, 24)

It may also be seen in our tendency to compartmentalize and seal off religious belief from everyday life. Patrick Keifert recounts the following (rather extreme) example of this tendency:

> Once, after I had spoken to a group of four hundred conservative Christians, a well-dressed man walked to the front, insistent on expressing his anger to me. He was particularly upset that I did not think Genesis 1 described the creation being completed in six twenty-four-hour days. I asked him what he did for a living. He replied that he had his Ph.D. in geological engineering and worked on the Iron Range in northern Minnesota. I asked him if he assumed in his everyday work that the earth was less than six thousand years old. He answered, 'No, that's what I pay you to do.'
> (Keifert 1992, 31)

A BARREN PUBLIC WORLD

Technopolis

Like Christianity, the Enlightenment was driven by an eschatological vision of a city. However, the city of reason was quite different from the city of God. At the end of the book of Revelation we are presented with a vision of a city with a garden at its very heart (Rev 22). The Christian vision was of an eschatological reconciliation of all that is now divided. From that city would flow healing for the nations – their reconciliation with God, but also their reconciliation with each other. In itself it would reunite the world of humankind and the world of nature.

By contrast the city of reason is a place where humankind has been adjusted to the machine. National divisions no longer create strife, because *Volksgeist* has finally been suppressed. There is no longer any conflict between humankind and nature, because nature has been excluded. The city of reason is the city of the machine.

The public world is the sphere of objective knowledge. One of the most persuasive contemporary advocates of the fact–value dichotomy, Karl Popper, has described this kind of knowledge as 'knowledge without a knower' (Popper 1972, 109). The subject has been excluded from the public world. Thus the city of reason is a place of impersonality.

The public world is also the sphere of production and economic facts. This is the rationalized world of mass production and Fordism. It is the realm of the factory and the office; the place of work. That, of course, is yet another modern dichotomy: the distinction between work and leisure – a distinction which would not have been recognized by our pre-modern forebears.

Functional rationality

Os Guinness reminds us that this 'is not a matter of "philosophical rationalism" but of "functional reality". In other words, reason used for practical rather than theoretical ends; reason as the servant of technology and development rather than of theology and philosophy' (Guinness 1983, 61).

It represents the institutionalization of Enlightenment rationalism in our social structures and public symbols. As I have already noted, the Enlightenment programme involves the reorganization of industry, commerce and government along more rational lines. Turning to our symbols, what is more characteristic of modernity than the clock? It is almost impossible to avoid clocks in any modern city. They are a permanent reminder that our public existence has been quantified and timetabled. Yevgeny Zamyatin paints the following dystopian picture of such a process taken to its ultimate conclusion:

> Each morning, with six-wheeled precision, at the very same minute and at the very same second we, in our millions, arise as one. At the very same hour we mono-millionedly begin

work – and, when we finish it, we do so mono-millionedly.
And merging into but one body with multi-millioned hands, at
the very second designated by the Tables of Hourly
Commandments we bring our spoons up to our mouths; at the
very same second, likewise, we set out for a walk, or go to an
auditorium, or the Hall of Taylor Exercises, or retire to
sleep.   (Zamyatin 1972, 28–9)

The public world is barren because the personal dimension of life
has been displaced. We are forced to seek elsewhere for personal
fulfilment. Thus under the conditions of modernity, personal
fulfilment entails a separation of role and identity. Where that does
not happen, where individuals continue to seek personal fulfilment
in the impersonal world of work, we find the characteristically
modern phenomenon of workaholism.

Similarly, because Christianity is fundamentally a personal
religion, it too was displaced from the public arena. Functional
rationality has as its corollary a functional secularism; a displacement of religion from the centre of life, not for ideological reasons,
but simply because our social structures cannot accommodate it.
This public secularism has resulted in a disenchantment of the world
far more radical than the Christian desacralization of the natural
world. And, of course, it implies the privatization of religion.

AN INTIMATE PRIVATE WORLD

The barren public world of modernity is, however, complemented
by a richly personal private world. Commentators often speak as if
the latter has been reduced to the status of an epiphenomenon. The
reality is more complex. At the very least, we should speak of the
complementarity of the two worlds rather than the subordination of
one to the other. Hegel's account of the master–slave relationship
may throw light on the relationship between the public and the
private spheres. They are in conflict; from the perspective of the
public ideology, public dominates and governs the private; but they
are inseparable. In modernity, the public and private spheres exist
in a symbiotic relationship: each provides something the other
lacks.

This private world is the realm of personal existence; the realm of
values, opinions and beliefs. As such it has become a refuge for
those aspects of human life which have proved less amenable to
rationalization.

The realm of personal freedom

The impersonality of the public world engenders a sense of powerlessness. In response to this we withdraw into a private world of leisure, family and religion. Here, in contrast to the rationalized determinism of the public realm, we find genuine freedom in the modern sense. Alone in our rooms we are free from the interference of others; free to do as we like.

A mark of this formal freedom is the sheer lack of structure in our private lives. The privatization of the family has meant that we lack significant role models upon which to base our family lives. Today most young adults embarking upon family life only have their own private experiences of privatized family life upon which to draw. Ironically, this lack of structure can actually prove a major hindrance in the quest for self-fulfilment or artistic self-expression. Without structures to guide us, how do we know where we are going or whether we are going anywhere? Today the quest for privatized self-fulfilment is rather like attempting to descend Ben Arthur in a white-out: one is aware, from the cries of those who have come to grief, that there are dangers which one cannot see; one is tempted to sit down and hope for the white-out to clear. Rollo May makes similar comments about the necessity of limits in artistic creativity:

> I propose that the statement, 'human possibilities are
> unlimited' is de-energizing . . . statements like this actually
> terrorize the listener: it is like putting someone into a canoe
> and pushing him out into the Atlantic toward England with the
> cheery comment, 'The sky's the limit.' The canoer is only too
> aware of the fact that an inescapably real limit is also the
> bottom of the ocean.   (May 1975, 112–13)

May continues by arguing that creativity requires limits as well as freedom. In order for artistic creativity to take place there has to be form as well as freedom: the artist needs the limitations imposed by the medium and the discipline of the techniques he or she has learned. Freedom understood as the mere absence of limitations is too negative and formal a concept of freedom to bear the weight put upon it by the privatization of so much of human life.

There is another point to note about this realm of personal freedom: it is bought at the price of public freedom. It is genuine freedom, but it is strictly circumscribed. By opting for a purely private personal freedom we become privatized people; we become the silent majority. Thus Os Guinness maintains that 'privatisation ultimately acts as a decisive limitation on freedom' (Guinness 1983, 78).

The realm of family life

Another major aspect of human life which has been privatized under modernity is family existence. Prior to industrialization the family was very much in the public arena. The family was the basic economic unit, with every member engaged in the activities which enabled the family as a whole to survive. The family was also considerably extended, with relationships criss-crossing the entire local community.

Urbanization and industrialization brought the death of the extended family. Its economic importance disappeared as family enterprises became uncompetitive in the face of the new rationalized factories with their division of labour and production lines.

A new privatized form of family existence emerged. As Theodore Roszak points out, by comparison with what it replaced, this was a much impoverished and truncated concept of family:

> The family as we know it is one of the most damaged and pathetic by-products of industrial upheaval . . . There should be a man to be drained of his full-time energy in the mill or the pit; a wife to keep his home, bear his children, and assume primary responsibility for their nurture (even when she might herself become a mill hand); children to be raised as the next generation of cheap labour. As an organizational base for the industrial system, the nuclear family was irreducible and utterly efficient, the smallest conceivable social entity that could man the factories and replenish the work force.
>
> (Roszak 1981, 159)

The realm of self-fulfilment and consumption

The separation of personal identity from public role means that modern men and women tend to seek their identities in the private sphere. Discovering myself and finding personal fulfilment have become leisure activities.

But, as Os Guinness has pointed out, the private realm is also the realm of consumption. Thus, in modernity, there is a fateful conjunction of consumption and the quest for self-fulfilment. This goes some way to explaining why so many of us actually seek self-fulfilment in consumption; the phenomenon of consumerism described earlier.

The realm of artistic expression

Yet another important aspect of being human which has been privatized by the modern world is that of artistic expression. Since aesthetic principles cannot be modelled upon empirical scientific lines they cannot count as public truth. As a result aesthetics has tended to be seen as no more than a matter of personal taste.

Since it is purely personal, it is also irrational and private. And Keifert points out that 'art can then become the expression of the individual artist. It does not need to be publicly available, nor does it serve public purposes' (Keifert 1992, 35).

This has other implications for art. For example, it results in the typically modern phenomenon of art divorced from action. Precisely because it is private and personal, the artistic creation need not address the public world. It also results in the idea of art for art's sake. From this perspective, art is 'answerable only to itself, has no social responsibility, and must not be evaluated according to the degree of correspondence it has to phenomena beyond itself, such as a moral order, the artist's intentions, or the circumstances of its production' (Begbie 1992, 62).

The realm of religion

Finally, there is the dramatic phenomenon of the displacement of religion from the very centre of public life to the private sphere. This privatization has been acquiesced in by modern Christians of both conservative and liberal outlooks. Its marks are not hard to spot.

The characteristic social structure of the modern privatized church is that of a voluntary association. It declares (albeit implicitly) in its constitution and the attitudes of its members that it is a private club for those whose leisure interest is religion. Some churches even exploit these characteristics for the sake of church growth.[6]

Spirituality in the privatized church is highly individualistic. It is a matter of my private pilgrimage with God, an encounter in a spiritual realm which is quite unconnected to politics, economics and science. In earlier generations, as Kenneth Leech has pointed out,

> Spirituality more and more came to be seen as an occupation for the leisured middle class, and for those with a special vocation to climb the higher steps of the spiritual ladder. For

the 'ordinary Christian' it was not seen as relevant.   (Leech 1993, 7)

As we proceed through the 1990s, spirituality is enjoying a revival. But, by and large, it remains the private leisure pursuit of individuals. Its expansion may have as much to do with an expansion of 'the leisured middle class' as with any serious rethinking of the nature of spirituality itself.

NOTES

1. The essay is clearly written with one eye upon the sensibilities of the Prussian authorities. He certainly goes out of his way to flatter the monarch, implying that he is enlightened and that he 'deserves to be esteemed by the grateful world and posterity as the first, at least from the side of government, who divested the human race of its tutelage' (Kant 1784).
2. On this showing, Kant would support those who call for the disciplining of liberal priests who express their views from the pulpit!
3. Of course the sheer power of the myths of progress and evolution led many to believe that national spiritualities were also subject to evolution. A particularly unpleasant example was the Nazi belief that a spiritual super-race (Hitler's *Herrnvolk*) would emerge from the Aryan *Volk*.
4. This is not to suggest that *no* hybridization occurs. Where else but in the USA could you find French–Japanese restaurants?
5. Of course this does not stop people from trying. Recent Western social thought is littered with such efforts, from Spencer's social Darwinism through the eugenics movement and Skinner's behaviourist utopia of *Walden Two* to the sociobiology of today.
6. As witness the contemporary church growth movement in North America and Great Britain.

PART II

WINDS OF CHANGE

CHAPTER 7

Modernity in Crisis

INTRODUCTION

For almost two centuries the public ideology of European and North American culture has been some variation of the modernity described in the preceding chapters. In its own terms modernity has been a highly successful cultural achievement.

Under the impact of modernity, Western society has seen massive changes in its social structures. Structures designed for a pre-industrial agrarian culture have largely given way to structures more appropriate for the technologically orientated urban living of today. Aristocratic feudal structures have given way to democratic or bureaucratic structures.

Even more dramatic than the sociological changes have been the technological changes. Driven by technological innovation, the modern era has been an era of exponential material progress. Twenty years ago, when I was an undergraduate in the physical sciences, we still used slide rules or table of logarithms to do calculations. Five years later, when I taught physics, my students were using pocket calculators more powerful than the desktop computers available when I was an undergraduate. Today my desktop computer (which is already obsolete) is more powerful than the university mainframes of the late 1960s. My grandmother was born before the début of the motor car and lived to see American astronauts land on the moon.

This technologically driven material progress has brought in its wake undoubted benefits. Greater material affluence has enabled the creation of public school systems which have led to unprecedented levels of literacy in the West. Medical care is more sophisticated and more widely available than it was a century ago. For all their well-debated flaws, the media of mass communication now available to ordinary men and women enable them to be much more aware of national and international events than was possible a generation or two ago.

Finally, the global expansion of modernity bears witness to its success. Between them, the capitalist and Marxist forms of modernity have had a major impact on every human culture in the twentieth century. The recent dramatic demise of Marxism has merely created a vacuum into which Western forms of modernity are flowing.

In spite of these undoubted successes, the last half-century has seen growing doubt about the wisdom of the modern experiment. Questions are raised about its social, psychological and spiritual implications. Critics suggest that the experiment has run its course. There are growing signs of dissatisfaction, instability and tension.

SIGNS OF A CRISIS

An addicted culture

Critics of modernity point out that it has resulted in an addicted culture. Addiction is not merely a personal problem, but a symptom of social or cultural dis-ease. As Kenneth Leech has pointed out:

> It is not possible to look at heroin and cocaine addiction
> without considering the wider context not only of deprivation
> and long term hopelessness about the future, but also of the
> economies of the Third World which depend heavily on opium
> and coca production. It is not possible to deal with problems
> raised by abuse of prescribed drugs without looking at the
> ethics of the pharmaceutical industry, and at the whole
> question of the dependence of our society on psychoactive
> chemicals to address personal needs.   (Leech 1993, 154–5)

However, drug and alcohol dependence are only the most obvious forms of addiction.[1] Our culture boasts several subtler (because socially approved) forms of addiction. At a personal level, one of the most significant is our addiction to activism. We live in a restless culture, a culture in which the workaholic is praised as a hero. It was Baudelaire, one of the nineteenth-century prophets of modernity, who commented that 'One must work, if not from taste then at least from despair. For, to reduce everything to a single truth: work is less boring than pleasure' (cited by Pieper 1952, 75).

I believe Baudelaire put his finger on a fundamental flaw in modernity. Medieval theologians would have identified it as the deadly sin of *acedia* or sloth. Far from mere laziness, this actually meant a refusal to be what we were created to be. Modernity's refusal to accept the finite creaturely status of human beings leads to restlessness, despair and work for work's sake. We cannot take pleasure in rest, because to rest is to admit our limitations.

Another subtle form of addiction in our culture may be our insistence on economic growth as the only sign of social health. As any doctor will point out, far from being the only sign of life, unregulated growth is a definition of cancer.

A violent culture

It is a commonplace that violence has become a characteristic of Western culture at every level.

Beginning with the individual, there appears to be a growing incidence of violence against the self (the most dramatic aspect being the rising incidence of suicide). More commonly, individuals direct their violence outwards into vandalism or violence against other people.

The daily news is full of stories of violence against others. We live in a society where crimes of violence are widespread. Violence is regarded by many as a legitimate means of obtaining certain goals. Thus we have the phenomenon of the terrorist who is prepared to injure or kill to achieve anything from a Marxist Ireland to equal rights for laboratory animals. Closely related to this is the rising tide of racist violence. Some individuals even seem to regard violence as pleasurable: abuse and murder have become forms of amusement.

More subtle forms of violence include the pornography industry and the phenomenon of media manipulation of consumer habits and voting patterns through advertising/propaganda. What does the advertising executive have in common with the serial killer who murders for pleasure? In both cases, normal personal relationships have given way to relationships of domination and control.

Violence is just as much in evidence at the international level. In spite of modern attempts to establish international forms of arbitration, diplomacy is still characterized by violence. Theodore

Roosevelt's dictum 'Speak softly and carry a big stick' sums up the general attitude: negotiation may be an opening gambit, but underlying the words is the threat of violence. In the twentieth century this international culture of violence has culminated in a nuclear arms race which has left the developed world with the capacity to destroy itself several times over. The present generation has been brought up in the shadow of 'overkill' and 'mutual assured destruction'. We may no longer perceive nuclear war as a threat, but that capacity for destruction remains. Furthermore, the *rapprochement* between East and West has not brought peace, but merely different enemies and a new era of high-tech warfare in which conventional weapons are used to create the kind of devastation formerly only obtainable from tactical nuclear weapons.

The environmental crisis

For many people in the West, the environmental crisis has now replaced the threat of nuclear war as the major threat to our continued existence. It is fitting to treat it separately, because it brings together both the addiction to economic growth and the violence of Western culture. Our addiction to economic growth regardless of the environmental costs has resulted in a frightening level of violence against nature. The statistics are too well known to require repeating here.

As with violence against individuals, property and other social, political or cultural groups, modern violence against nature is rooted in an attitude of domination.

The crisis itself is a salutary reminder of the finitude of the environment we inhabit. As Walter Wink points out:

> We can plunder, ravage, poison, and imbalance the ecology all we want, yet in the very act of spoiling our nest we are at every moment sustained by means of the life-giving nutrients and energies the ecology is still able to provide. But the ecology is not mocked. There comes a point of irreversibility when the poisons we dump become our own drink, and we come under the 'judgment' of the ecosystem.   (Wink 1984, 64–5)

The environmental crisis has served notice that there are real physical limits to the growth that is possible. It also calls into question our faith in the omnipotence of technology. Thus this crisis strikes at the most fundamental myths of modernity.

Families under pressure

It is perhaps inevitable that a book written for a twentieth-century Christian readership would include as a crisis of modernity the contemporary pressure on family life. Again, the statistics of divorce, family breakdown and child abuse speak for themselves.

However, the conventional wisdom of pro-family campaigners, that the institution of the family is undervalued in modernity, is almost certainly wrong. The divorce statistics are swollen by men and women who have just broken up with their third, fourth or fifth wife or husband. If the family is undervalued, why do so many people persist in trying to establish themselves in a family?

Far from being undervalued, I suggested in the last chapter that the stress on intimacy within the private sphere created by modernity actually overvalues families. Since it is the primary social structure of the private sphere, the family has been idealized. At the same time, that very privatization has cut families off from possible models and has contributed to a lack of structure within family life. The combination of high expectations with few structures or models is a recipe for instability.

THE FAILURE OF MODERNITY

The world-view or symbolic universe of modernity no longer satisfies. In recent generations it has been questioned at a number of basic points. This may be illustrated by looking at some of the typical functions of a world-view. A satisfactory world-view provides its adherents with, among other things, a basis for what constitutes knowledge, a set of cultural norms (maps of reality and morality), emotional security and a way of controlling cultural change. As the preceding chapters have attempted to show, modernity has in the past offered all of these to the Western world. Today, however, many people who have been brought up with the assumptions of modernity are calling them into question.

Science and meaninglessness

Modernity has glorified objectivity and detachment at the expense of relatedness and involvement. However, scientific detachment has proved to be an ambiguous virtue.

Over the past century the older optimistic vision of the scientist as omniscient spectator has given way to a very different perspective. Instead of conferring divine status, detachment and objectivity are increasingly perceived as consigning us to alienation. Thus one twentieth-century philosopher of science sees in Descartes' achievement

> the first stage in the reading of man quite out of the real and primary realm. His was a life of colours and sounds, of pleasures, of griefs, of passionate loves. Hence the real world must be the world outside of man . . . Man begins to appear for the first time in the history of thought as an irrelevant spectator and insignificant effect of the great mathematical system which is the substance of reality.   (E. A. Burtt cited by Barbour 1966, 34)

One man's divine detachment is another's demonic alienation. This change of perspective may be explained by exploring the effect of the modern combination of a mechanistic cosmos with a rationalistic insistence on the sufficiency of explanations couched in terms of finite causes.

It is a characteristic of mechanisms that their purpose is external to them: they are meaningless in themselves. This was what gave Paley's analogy of the watch its plausibility for generations of natural theologians. If the world can be demonstrated to be a mechanism, it follows that its purpose must be external and this, in turn, suggests the existence of a creator whose purposes it serves. The pointlessness of the physical cosmos can be suppressed by the retention of a spiritual purpose for humankind. In a dualistic world-view, the physical universe may be meaningless while the spiritual world retains meaning and purpose. However, in our century there has been a widespread reaction against such a response.

An alternative, and more consistent, naturalistic response would be to say that the world has no purpose whatsoever. Such is the view of many who have contemplated the universe from the perspective of modern scientific naturalism. Thus, 'The more the universe seems comprehensible, the more it also seems pointless' (Weinberg 1977, 154). Or, as P.W. Atkins puts it:

> We are the children of chaos, and the deep structure of change is decay. At root there is only corruption, and the un-stemmable tide of chaos. Gone is purpose: all that is left is direction. This is the bleakness we have to accept as we peer deeply and dispassionately into the heart of the Universe.
>
> (cited by Newbigin 1990, 1)

Picking up a phrase suggested by yet another scientist, Loren Eiseley, we have become 'cosmic orphans', alone in an uncaring impersonal material universe.

Knowledge as power

Reason, in the narrow modern sense of the term epitomized by Bacon's aphorism, is concerned with means rather than ends; with ways of achieving things rather than truth. Furthermore, it implicitly denies rational status to purposes and ends. Hence the apparent meaninglessness of a cosmos rendered transparent by scientific investigation.

Nietzsche was the first to point out another implication of this approach to reason. He took Bacon at face value: knowledge is power *and nothing more*. It is a matter of creating order by imposing an interpretation upon the otherwise unintelligible flux of Becoming. This process of creating meaning in a meaningless universe is an expression of the will to power. It is not a matter of truth, but of the invention of useful fictions.

But to whom are they useful? Nietzsche shone the spotlight of suspicion upon the absolute truths of philosophy and religion and revealed, to his satisfaction, a network of fictions created by one interest group to subjugate another.

In similar vein, the contemporary cultural commentator David Harvey points out that

> The moral crisis of our time is a crisis of Enlightenment thought . . . the Enlightenment affirmation of 'self without God' in the end negated itself because reason, a means, was left, in the absence of God's truth, without any spiritual or moral goal. If lust and power are 'the only values that don't need the light of reason to be discovered,' then reason had to become a mere instrument to subjugate others.   (Harvey 1990, 41)

The result is a pervasive suspicion of truth claims in contemporary culture. If knowledge is power, and power corrupts, then absolute knowledge corrupts absolutely.

The aridity of information

Another point at which modernity has lost its enchantment for many of our contemporaries is its tendency to reductionism:

everything intelligent beings do, not just their thinking, is purely and simply a form of information processing. It follows that every conceivable thought and action of any possible form of life is ultimately constrained by the physical laws governing the processing of information.   (Barrow and Tipler 1986, 660)

In common with many modern men and women, these well-known physicists make it clear that they believe that all human thought can be reduced to so many bits of quantitative information. However, this emphasis on quantifiability is yet another reminder of the aridity of the public world of modernity: a world where the qualitative concept of trustworthiness is reduced to the quantifiable concept of credit status.

> Where is the wisdom we have lost in knowledge?
> Where is the knowledge we have lost in information?
> (T.S. Eliot, *Choruses from 'The Rock'*, I)

We are left with a colourless, tasteless public world of scientific data and economic information.

Too many choices: plurality or fragmentation?

Western consumerism has resulted in a bewildering variety of choices on the supermarket shelves. Today, when we go shopping, we have to make far more decisions than our parents or grandparents. That innocent-looking item, washing powder, conceals a minefield: which of the thirty-odd brands should I get? Should I get its original non-biological, biological or ultra-concentrated form? Should I, indeed, get it as a liquid? And virtually every purchasing decision we make is now cloaked in similar complexities.

As I pointed out in the last chapter, private plurality means that there is an equally bewildering freedom of choice available in the arts, entertainment and belief systems.[2]

The question arises, what happens when a person is faced with too many decisions? One response is to take refuge in authority. The guru or charismatic prophet will tell you what to think, how to dress, perhaps even who to marry and how to vote. Another option is indecision (or agnosticism). Yet another possibility is to make an arbitrary decision. In effect, one abandons reason in favour of will to power.

This multiplicity of choice raises a number of questions about modernity's continued functioning as a world-view.

A world-view offers emotional security. This is the acceptable face of what Kant dismissed as tutelage: our dependence on the community in which we are brought up for so many of our assumptions and beliefs. Human beings are afraid of freedom – and rightly so – when that freedom amounts to a lack of structures which give our lives shape and meaning. But, as Nietzsche pointed out so effectively, the world-view of modernity contained within it the seeds of its own destruction. It has cast us adrift in an ocean without distinguishing features:

> How were we able to drink up the sea? Who gave us the sponge to wipe away the entire horizon? What did we do when we unchained this earth from its sun? Whither is it moving now? Whither are we moving now? Away from all suns? Are we not perpetually falling? Backward, sideward, forward, in all directions? Is there any up or down left?
>
> Are we not straying as through an infinite nothing? Do we not feel the breath of empty space? Has it not become colder?   (Nietzsche 1977, 202–3)

Implicit in the modern world-view is a denial of all that provides us with emotional security. Small wonder that, in the twentieth century, modernity has increasingly been characterized by violence, addiction and loss of hope.

A world-view also typically offers cultural norms: maps of reality and morality which function as an important unifying factor in society. Here, too, the modern world-view appears to contain the seeds of its own destruction. The relativism to which I have referred indicates that there is no longer agreement on these cultural norms.

Finally, a world-view is usually expected to limit cultural change. But, far from controlling it, there is an aspect of modernity which actually encourages change. Again, Baudelaire highlights this with his comment that 'Modernity is the transient, the fleeting, the contingent' (cited by Harvey 1990, 10). As one sociologist has pointed out,

> we have reached the stage in pluralisation where choice is not just a state of affairs, it is a state of mind. Choice has become a value in itself, even a priority. To be modern is to be addicted to choice and change. Change becomes the very essence of life.   (Guinness 1983, 100)

But, if one of the chief values of modernity is change, and all that is of personal value has been walled up in the relativistic realm of the private, there is nothing to stop runaway change and fragmentation.

RESPONDING TO THE CRISIS IN MODERNITY

As we explore contemporary Western culture, we discover a wide range of responses to the perceived crisis.

Denial

Inevitably there are those who refuse to admit the existence of such a crisis. Even quite recently, the liberal establishment was prepared to cast doubt upon the reality of the environmental crisis. Typical would be Simon and Kahn's response to the *Global 2000 Report* (Simon and Kahn 1984). Among other things, they argued that global life expectancy is increasing, global birth rates are falling, deforestation is not a problem, there is no evidence of increased extinction, there is no evidence of climatic change, nuclear power is cheaper and cleaner than coal/oil, and the pollution threat is exaggerated. They insisted that 'the nature of the physical world permits continued improvement in humankind's economic lot in the long run, indefinitely' (Simon and Kahn 1984, 3).

A similar denial of the crisis may be seen in Francis Fukuyama's recent pronouncements about the ideological victory of capitalism over communism. As far as he is concerned, there are simply no viable alternatives to the Western form of modernity. The collapse of Marxism represents 'the end of history as such: that is, the end point of mankind's ideological evolution and the universalization of Western liberal democracy as the final form of human government' (Fukuyama 1989, 4).

Blame-shifting

An alternative to denial is to shift the blame. The more realistic of the liberal ideologues are prepared to admit that Western culture faces major problems. However, they deny that these problems are related to modernity itself.

For example, a recurring theme of right-wing politicians during the last decade has been the demise of family values. But, instead of recognizing that the pressures on the family come from modernity itself, they prefer to scapegoat the Church: Church of England bishops are accused of failing to give a moral lead to the nation.

A similar strategy can sometimes be observed in attempts to trace the historical roots of the environmental crisis. Lynn White's famous essay on 'The historical roots of our ecologic crisis' put the blame firmly upon Western Christianity (White, 1967). Subsequently some Christian writers have attempted to shift the blame from their particular Christian tradition to another.

The rejection of the West

A third strategy which has proved popular has been the rejection of Western culture altogether. Many people, disillusioned with modernity, have sought alternative (more spiritual) ways of understanding the world in the highways and byways of Eastern mysticism.

At the same time there has been a resurgence of non-Western culture. The most dramatic example of this is surely the re-emergence of Islam as a world power. In the post-Marxist realignment of world politics, it certainly seems to be the case that the West (now including most of the former Eastern Bloc nations) is united in its opposition to Islam (especially Iran, Iraq and Libya).

Beyond modernity

A fourth option might be called the radicalization of modernity. When Nietzsche penned his purple prose about the death of God, he was not calling upon people to despair. Nietzsche is widely described as a nihilist, but, unlike his mentor Schopenhauer, his was a profoundly optimistic nihilism: nihilism with a smile. Instead of despair, he called people to have the courage to replace God: to become the creators of their own meanings and realities. Today that Nietzschean sentiment has become an essential part of postmodernity.

NOTES

1. Of course, many religious traditions have used drugs to elicit spiritual experiences. A similar process may be visible in the spread of drug abuse among sections of the population not traditionally thought of as at risk. For a technique-dominated society, a drug such as LSD offers instantaneous 'spiritual' experience without the inconvenience of religious commitment. Designer drugs effectively offer our culture a consumer spirituality!
2. Always provided, of course, one has the money to exercise freedom of choice.

CHAPTER 8

The Self-Destruction
of Reasoning

THE ENLIGHTENMENT'S PYRRHIC VICTORY

In Chapter 2 I suggested that the Enlightenment project was driven by a vision of the rational society. I also began to explore the extent to which that vision had reshaped Western culture in the modern era. It would not be an exaggeration to say that our culture has indeed come to be driven by a particular understanding of reason. However, the success of the Enlightenment project in this respect has not been without its costs. One wonders how many of the founding fathers of the Enlightenment would recognize our culture as the child of their vision.

The dominance of technical reason

In pre-modern Western philosophy, reason was understood to be the faculty of the mind whereby we grasp and transform reality. As Paul Tillich points out, it was a far broader concept than modern understandings of reason: 'It is effective in the cognitive, aesthetic, practical, and technical functions of the human mind. Even emotional life is not irrational in itself' (Tillich 1951, 72). Thus reason embraced both cognitive and non-cognitive aspects of the human mind.

However, the non-cognitive dimension of reason has been effectively suppressed by the social process of rationalization which has followed in the wake of the Enlightenment. It became the norm to dismiss these aspects as irrational or subjective.[1] For example, dreams, which were formerly regarded as significant, were now dismissed as nonsense. Thus Wilhelm Wundt, a pioneer of experimental psychology, regarded them as a form of illusion. Even Freud, whose use of dream analysis is well known, seems to have accepted this negative assessment, treating them primarily as a mine of repressed memories.

The suppression of the non-cognitive aspects of reason was accompanied by an exclusive emphasis on technical reason (or reasoning). The sheer power of this approach in enabling us to manipulate the world is unquestioned. However, the very exclusiveness of modernity's emphasis upon technical reason has a number of important implications.

Some of those implications have already been touched on in Chapter 2. For example, although technical reason properly involves both analysis and synthesis, there is a tendency to put greater stress on the former element. The elements of a phenomenon are regarded as what is really there, whereas the patterns and wholes we discern are treated as mental constructs, useful tools which may or may not correspond to reality. Walter Wink has suggested that this tendency is implicitly religious. In deciding to treat the irreducible components of nature as ultimate reality, modern science was unwittingly embracing the classical idolatry of the elements (*stoicheia*) which is referred to in Colossians 2.8. He describes the tendency to reductionism as 'a religious instinct made fanatical and demonic by its severance from its divine ground and its total isolation in matter' (Wink 1986, 139).

But, even within the limits of technical reason, analysis is not the whole story. As Tolkien comments through the mouth of Gandalf the Grey: 'he that breaks a thing to find out what it is has left the path of wisdom' (Tolkien 1954, 272). Analysis alone leaves only broken parts. The dissecting table may yield valuable insights, but it is not the whole truth about the creature we have killed to obtain those insights. Analysis needs to be balanced by a synthetic or holistic perspective.

However, the modern fascination with reasoning has further and more subtle implications. Tillich has pointed out that our single-minded insistence on technical reason actually has the effect of distorting technical reason itself. This is because our concentration neglects the larger framework within which technical reason operates. The very structure of technical reason depends upon presuppositions which are not based on technical reason (Tillich 1951, 73).

Perhaps one of the most serious implications of an exclusive emphasis on technical reason is the exclusion of ends from our reasoning. Technical reason is concerned only with the means. Thus the pursuit of knowledge in the modern era is divorced from the uses to which it might be put. Furthermore, the discussion of those uses or ends is beyond the pale of the new and limited sphere of reason.

But if ends or purposes are not within the purview of reason (as understood today), where are they to be found?

Reasoning and domination

Closely related to the triumph of technical reason is the triumph of human autonomy over the various external authorities which governed pre-modern humankind. Most significantly, our ends are no longer given by God, by the transcendent *Logos*, by the eternal ground of order and reason. Since the Enlightenment the self has been declared sovereign: we are the creators of our own ends and purposes.

However, the modern divorce of reasoning from a larger concept of reason has had the effect of denying rational status to those ends. As Nietzsche graphically demonstrated a century ago, the effect is to reduce our arguments to expressions of the will to power.[2] Thus technical reason is a tool which has, in our age, often been used to dominate others.

In Chapter 3 I introduced the objectifying tendency of the Cartesian and Newtonian approaches to reality. The point made so effectively by Nietzsche and many others is that this has not stopped with the natural world. It is precisely by treating others as objects that we seek to subjugate them to our will. Guided only by the irrational force of the will to power, technical reason inevitably becomes a dehumanizing force.

But the realization that technical reason is an apt tool for dominating others has further implications. If we suspect that truth claims are covert claims to power, we will be inclined to be sceptical about those truth claims. This has led to the postmodern denial of public truth. Attempts to articulate a coherent world-view are dismissed as inherently repressive or illusory.

Scepticism about the truth of language also implies that language ceases to refer to anything beyond itself. Again, this tendency can be seen clearly in postmodernism, where the emphasis is on the signifier rather than the signified. It is seen in the characteristically postmodern use of montage: the juxtaposition of unrelated images from quite separate worlds of discourse is not intended as an argument, but rather is intended to produce an immediate non-rational effect (an aesthetic orgasm). Or again, it may be seen in the characteristically postmodern form of literary criticism (not to mention historiography and philosophical discourse), namely, deconstruction. The deconstructionist is not interested in the arguments or intentions of the author, but rather in the covert forms of repression which may be discerned from the text.

The modernist response to such a denial of truth claims can only be one of nihilism and despair. The situation in which we find ourselves represents the final frustration of modernity's utopian visions, the stark denial of a hoped-for future. That relatively few people in our culture have finally abandoned themselves to such despair is perhaps an indication that there really is a cultural sea change taking place. David Harvey suggests that the characteristic psychopathology of postmodernity is neither despair nor paranoia. Despair entails a relatively coherent sense both of self and of a future that is now beyond reach. According to Harvey, the postmodernist avoids despair because he or she lacks that degree of coherence: the world of the postmodernist is essentially schizophrenic (Harvey 1990, 53).

Where can wisdom be found?

In one sense the Enlightenment project has been highly successful. It has created a culture based upon technical reason. But the result is anything but the humane society guided by reason which the philosophers of the Enlightenment anticipated. On the contrary, in the very act of triumphing over a broader classical view of reason, technical reason has destroyed itself (or at least its own credibility).

It now appears that the base upon which the utopian visions of modernity were founded was far too narrow. One might say that, in pursuing a vision of en*light*enment, modernity has ignored or suppressed the shadow-side of existence. I have already noted that it was an unrealistically optimistic vision, in that it denied the existence of radical evil. But, by ignoring the entirely legitimate non-cognitive dimensions of human existence, it has produced a seriously impoverished vision of what it is to be human. Small wonder that fictional attempts to portray the rational society have usually taken the form of dystopias rather than utopias. Small wonder that Fukuyama's eulogy on the final victory of modernity (in its Western liberal form) has more than a hint of the epitaph about it: much that we regard as best in humankind (e.g. courage, idealism and imagination) will be 'replaced by economic calculation, the endless solving of technical problems, environmental concerns, and the satisfaction of sophisticated consumer demands' (Fukuyama 1989, 18).

BEYOND REASON

The Romantic reaction

Before modernity had even achieved the status of public ideology, the impoverishment of its vision had already been recognized and a powerful reaction had set it (in some quarters). This reaction took the form of Romanticism, a powerful artistic and philosophical movement which released and celebrated much that had been suppressed by the philosophers of the Enlightenment.

In contrast to the Enlightenment, which might be called a philosophy of reason, Romanticism was a philosophy of imagination (Tillich 1967, 81). It sought to reverse the Enlightenment at a number of crucial points. For example, in contrast to the Enlightenment's emphasis on technical reason, the Romantics stressed the epistemological importance of intuition: intuition was regarded as the faculty by which we grasp the infinite in the finite.

Romanticism also stressed the value of history, tradition and hierarchical authority against the Enlightenment charge that they tyrannized humankind. Given the socio-economic status of the spokesmen of Romanticism, it could easily be seen as the conservative reaction of an aristocratic creative élite against the egalitarianism of Enlightenment thought.

Perhaps most important was Romanticism's espousal of the *Volksgeist*, the unique and irreducible spirit of a people, against the levelling universalizing effects of the Enlightenment. As I have already pointed out, this had a major impact on the development of nationalism and cultural pluralism.

However, Romanticism was permitted only relative freedom within modern culture. Both by virtue of its character as a reaction and because of the visible success of modernity, Romanticism operated within limits set by the dominant outlook. Thus Romantic ideas were allowed free rein in the private sphere while being ruthlessly suppressed in the public sphere. To take just one example, Goethe's theory of colour (a major Romantic riposte to the dominant Newtonian view) was rejected out of hand by the scientific community.

Explorations inwards

Within the limits imposed by the public ideology, Romanticism did permit many people within our culture to begin exploring those territories of mind and spirit which the Enlightenment had neglected. So closely related were Romanticism and the nineteenth-century explosion of interest in spirituality that Romanticism has been described as 'the cultural movement which encompasses the modern Gnostic advance' (Raschke 1980, 51).

Among the multiplicity of new paganisms which erupted at this time, one or two stand out as of lasting significance. One of the most influential was undoubtedly the Theosophical Society, founded by Helena Blavatsky. Although its formal membership has never been large, it is the fountainhead from which literally hundreds of esoteric spiritual groups have sprung in the past century. In Victorian England it provided an exotic spiritual path which was sufficiently attractive for Annie Besant to abandon her post as vice-president of the National Secular Society. It has also had a remarkable (though hardly benign) political influence in our century. Its evolutionary spirituality was one of the elements which fed into the emergence of Nazism as a spiritual and political force, while its staunch advocacy of Hindu beliefs provided considerable encouragement for the development of twentieth-century neo-Hinduism.[3]

Another Romantic spiritual movement was the revival of ritual magic; the most notable example being the Hermetic Order of the Golden Dawn. Founded by the brother-in-law of the philosopher Henri Bergson, Golden Dawn was another breeding ground of nationalism (in this case, Irish and Scottish). Again, its members have had an influence on twentieth-century spirituality quite out of proportion to their numbers. The leading theorist of the movement was none other than W.B. Yeats. C.S. Lewis's friend Charles Williams was a member, and, for a short time, so was the great Christian mystic Evelyn Underhill. On the pagan side, the most influential member was undoubtedly Aleister Crowley, a key figure in modern occultism.

In addition to these direct and privatized explorations of the spiritual realm, the twentieth century has seen the beginning of more 'scientific' forays into this world. I am thinking particularly of the work of people like Freud and Jung rather than experimental psychology. It is doubtful whether their work can be called scientific in the narrower ideological sense of the word. However, the term does highlight the fact that they have attempted a disciplined application of technical reason to the contents of dreams, fantasies, mythology and spirituality.

The most recent development in this area is the emergence of the New Age movement. Ranging from crass commercialism and dubious psychotechnologies to disciplined spiritualities and sophisticated forms of psychoanalysis, this incredibly diverse phenomenon signals a widespread dissatisfaction with the public ideology of modernity. As modernity loses its grip on Western culture, these semi-private alternatives are becoming increasingly respectable and influential. It is not so much that they are taking over the public arena, but rather that the public ideology of the West has atrophied to such an extent that it no longer exercises its former strict control on the public–private demarcation.

Affirming the non-rational

A century of such explorations of the unconscious has borne fruit in the contemporary questioning of modernity's prejudice against the non-rational. Today many voices would echo Hamlet's 'There are more things in heaven and earth, Horatio, than are dreamt of in your philosophy'.

Of course modernity is well-equipped with arguments against the non-rational. Warnings that we are opening the floodgates of superstition and irrationality abound. Invidious comparisons with the ideology of Nazism are used in an effort to frighten people into maintaining the modern status quo. The hermeneutics of suspicion which has been used so effectively against technical reason can very easily be turned against non-rational forms of knowledge: they too can be dismissed as covert claims to power. And the New Age movement, in particular, is such a mixed bag that the witch-hunters of modernity can find ample fuel to stoke their bonfires.

Nevertheless, what we are seeing today is a growing recognition that there are other ways to elicit knowledge than by the methods of technical reason. It is increasingly being realized that technical reason must be complemented by non-cognitive mental processes.

One common way of expressing this complementarity is by means of Robert Ornstein's theory of hemispheres. In its original form this was a psychological theory based upon the behaviour of patients who had undergone major brain surgery. It was found that the two halves or hemispheres of the brain functioned autonomously and were responsible for different activities. For example, it was found that the right hemisphere of the brain controlled motion on the left side of the body and vice versa. It was also found that the left hemisphere controlled speech.

This theory has been generalized and is now widely used to relate psychological functions to hemispheres. Thus the articulate left hemisphere is regarded as the seat of our rational, analytical, systematizing powers. Conversely, the inarticulate right hemisphere is the seat of our emotions, intuition, sexuality and creativity. Interestingly, the functions ascribed to the left hemisphere are those which in Western society have been associated with the male, with culture, with all that is finest in us. The functions associated with the right hemisphere correspond to what Western society has dismissed or condemned as feminine, irrational, or bestial. This theory represents an internalization of these dualisms. It implies that they can be transcended within the person by recognizing them as complementary rather than contradictory.

It is now commonplace to hear people warning that Western culture has relied too heavily on the very obvious powers of the left hemisphere. We have become obsessed with one aspect of the brain's functions at the expense of allowing other functions to atrophy. In order to overcome our personal and social crises we must seek ways of improving communication between the two hemispheres. Left and right brain are complementary. Reason and emotion; analysis and intuition of the whole; ordinary and altered states of consciousness: we need them all if we are to function fully as human beings. That is the new ideal.

THE WAY OF TRUST

Reason under the domination system

In his trilogy on the theology of power, Walter Wink argues that all of reality is dipolar, with both an outward manifestation in material and social structures and a corresponding inward manifestation or spirit. He identifies the principalities and powers of biblical language with 'the actual spirituality at the center of the political, economic, and cultural institutions' (Wink 1992, 6) of the authors' day. Further, he argues that the 'world' against which the authors of the New Testament warn us is not the material world, but rather the world system comprising ungodly structures together with their spiritual dimension. Thus when Jesus said 'I am not of this world' (John 8.23), he was not claiming to be an otherworldly spirit, but denying that he belonged to the godless world system to which the Pharisees had accommodated themselves.

Looking for a single word to characterize the world system, Wink has hit upon domination. The characteristics of that system as described by Wink bear an uncanny resemblance to those aspects of modernity which have been called into question in preceding chapters. Thus an alternative way of looking at the preceding account of the triumph and self-destruction of technical reason would be to see it as the history of the adaptation of reason to such a system. It is the exclusive use of one particular type of reason: that type of reason which is particularly well adapted to the task of control and manipulation. Technical reason has become reason in the service of idolatrous ends.

Reason under conditions of participation

Contemporary dissatisfaction with technical reason and the entire world-view of modernity may be a sign of hope. It is certainly an opportunity to encourage people to entertain alternatives.

The alternative which Wink suggests was first posed by Jesus of Nazareth might be called the participation system (or, more traditionally, the kingdom of God). In this system, personhood is defined not by autonomy, as it is in modernity and the domination system, but by personal relationship. The kind of knowledge which is characteristic of this system will be rooted in trust; it will not have been wrested from the other by an impersonal application of technical reason.

Such knowledge will be dipolar; a function of both the known and the knower. Without doubt the most important exploration of this alternative was that undertaken by Michael Polanyi. Polanyi was a Hungarian-born chemist who was deeply dissatisfied with the impersonality and detachment of the modern approach to reason, and in later life became a philosopher in order to advocate the *'personal participation* of the knower in all acts of understanding' (Polanyi 1958, vii).

For Polanyi, our knowledge grows out of the soil of what he calls tacit knowledge. This is the everyday, commonsense, implicit knowledge which all of us possess. Polanyi used to introduce the concept by saying 'we know more than we can tell'. A mother knows the cry of her baby in the midst of an entire maternity ward. We recognize each other (even if we have not met for years, our hairstyle has changed and we have lost weight), but we cannot say how we know: there is a *gestalt* which cannot simply be programmed into a computer. We recognize the letter 'a' whether it appears in Roman, italic, Gothic or sans serif script: by contrast, computers equipped with optical character recognition hardware and software still have to be programmed to recognize each individual type of script. Competent drivers do so tacitly: we would not feel particularly secure if we thought the driver made a conscious effort to remember where the brake pedal was every time he or she wished to slow down!

Another way in which Polanyi expressed this characteristic of knowledge was by means of the tactile metaphor of indwelling (as opposed to detachment). Indwelling refers to the personal appropriation of knowledge, the bringing of it into 'organic relationship with the rest of the person's body of knowledge' so that it 'becomes an extension of the self, a tool for further exploration of reality' (Scott 1985, 73). Lady Scott cites the example of an Oxford University Press compositor who, although he knew no Sanskrit, was able to spot a typographical error in a Sanskrit text. She explains: 'He had got used to the regular patterns of the arm movements that he made as his hand moved from one compartment to another to pick up the type, and he was alerted by a move that was different' (Scott 1985, 72). He did not understand the text, but he recognized that a particular combination of letters was so unusual as to be a possible error.

Knowledge rooted in this soil will be fallible. Again, this is common sense. But it contrasts sharply with the Cartesian obsession with absolute certainty. Polanyi has rejected Descartes' search for certainty in favour of a commitment to reality. At the very heart of knowing is an act of faith, a recognition that I might be mistaken and a preparedness to take the risk of error in order that I might know.

Such knowledge will also be incomplete. This implies that it is dynamic: continued learning is an essential part of the system. Since there can be no absolute certainty, we must remain open both to what we already believe we know and to reality. It demands trust: trust in our experience and in the relationships, community and tradition which have shaped us. It also demands a readiness to change in response to new discoveries about reality.

Although knowledge is a function of the knower, this does not mean it is subjective. Fear of subjectivity drove modernity towards an objective knowledge which has proved, in the end, to be dehumanizing. For Polanyi, the openness to reality of which I have spoken involves a reaching beyond self to the other. It is relational knowledge: a knowledge based on acquaintance with the other (a knowledge which may, of course, be refined by reasoning).

Personal knowledge is also relational in the sense that it is never the exclusive property of an individual. A completely private belief does not count as knowledge. On the contrary, only when I am prepared to commit myself to public action on the basis of what I believe can that belief be regarded as knowledge. In one of his novels Chaim Potok asserts that 'If a person has a contribution to make, he must make it in public. If learning is not made public, it is a waste' (Potok 1970, 148). Polanyi himself used to cite the example of Christopher Columbus: many people besides Columbus were prepared to speculate about the possibility of the earth being round. Only Columbus was prepared to stake his life and reputation on the reality of a round earth.

NOTES

1. One of the hallmarks of post-Enlightenment thought is the tendency to equate subjective with irrational (or even unreal). It is no coincidence that this tendency is commonplace among fundamentalist writers.
2. And, one might add with a nod in the direction of Freud, to lust or libido.
3. Theosophy has been cited as one of the formative influences on the VHP (Vishva Hindu Parishad), the religious wing of contemporary Hindu fundamentalism (Aagard 1982).

CHAPTER 9

Absolute Relativism

THE PROGRESS OF RELATIVISM

Pragmatic relativism

Modernity tamed the Romantic resurgence of the private sphere by the selective employment of relativism. The public sphere retained its dominance over the private as long as the truths of the former were granted a universality denied to those of the private sphere.

This pragmatic use of relativism may still be seen in the public education systems of the West. As Ivan Illich has pointed out:

> The school system today performs the threefold function common to powerful churches throughout history. It is simultaneously the repository of society's myth, the institutionalization of that myth's contradictions, and the locus of the ritual which reproduces and veils the disparities between myth and reality.   (Illich 1971, 43)

Thus one would expect our education systems to be dominated by the ideology of secular liberalism. Implicit in this domination will be certain assumptions about what constitutes knowledge and how it is to be imparted. The Conservative government's espousal of 'traditional standards of education' constitutes a particularly crude example of these assumptions. Thus a premium is placed on scientific models of understanding; knowledge is quantified and reduced to information (e.g. John Major's insistence that history does involve a knowledge of dates). However, the modern methods to which the government objects are, in reality, no more pluralistic. They pay lip service to our multicultural situation, but they do not allow other cultures to challenge their liberal assumptions in any fundamental way. Thus 'multicultural' education tends to concentrate only on what is non-threatening in other cultures (e.g. music, food, dress, and customs), while shying away from critical questions which those cultures might address to our own.

That the pluralism or relativism of our education system is superficial may be seen by the fact that when faced with religious or philosophical systems which call it into question it resorts to debunking. True relativism would not attempt to defend itself against alternative belief systems. It would simply assert that alternatives are incommensurable, that they cannot be compared. But, in fact, educationalists (and others) are quite prepared to defend their corner against, e.g. conservative Christians or Muslims.

Pragmatic relativism has proved a powerful weapon in maintaining the dominance of the public sphere with its content of classical science and economics. However, relativism is a dangerous weapon for those who use it: it is sharper than any sword, and apt to find the throat of its wielder!

Ideological relativism

In contrast to such pragmatism, ideological relativism asserts that there is no ultimate frame of reference for our beliefs. There are no universals. World-views are strictly incommensurable: they can no more be compared than, say, music and fishcakes. They are unrelated language games which can only be meaningful to the participants.

This does not mean that there is no such thing as truth. There may be truth and falsehood within the context of a particular world-view. The criterion for truth or falsehood becomes coherence: is this assertion consistent with the fundamental assumptions of this world-view?

For the relativist, each culture or community of belief has its own values and canons of truth. At any one time, different cultures will espouse different values; they will see the world in different ways. There is no universal canon of human reason, and therefore no basis for the Enlightenment vision of a global rational society.

Truth and values also differ within the history of any given culture. Thus ideological relativism entails a historicist reading of history. As we have already seen, this was the interpretation of history inspired by the Romantic reaction against the cultural imperialism of the Enlightenment. The belief that truth and values change with time has serious consequences for post-Enlightenment thought. It implies that it is no longer possible to define a single goal for cultural evolution. Thus there is no longer any basis for the Enlightenment belief in progress. Furthermore, since different historical eras and cultures are strictly incommensurable with our own, it implies that both the study of history and the study of other cultures involve an empathetic leap. Thus history and anthropology are not strictly rational disciplines. To the extent that we take such disciplines seriously, we call into question the hegemony of technical reason.

The departure of ideological relativism from the canons of the Enlightenment is seen most clearly in contemporary sociological treatments of science. This citadel of modernity is now besieged by the forces of postmodernity. In these critiques of Enlightenment science it is argued that, far from being representations of reality, scientific theories are tools which give power to the community that has constructed them. The impression is sometimes given that science is a conspiracy of white bourgeois males against women, or the proletariat or the oppressed peoples of the Third World! In other words, the truths of science may be true for members of the scientific community, but their universality is called into question and modernity's efforts to impose them on the rest of the world are seen as an exercise in cultural domination rather than education.

THE MAKING OF A PLURALISTIC SOCIETY

According to Os Guinness, pluralization is 'the process by which the number of options in the private sphere of modern society rapidly multiplies at all levels, especially at the level of world views, faiths and ideologies' (Guinness 1983, 96).

But what forces in our culture have contributed to the formation of today's undeniably pluralistic society?

The rapid urbanization of Western culture during the nineteenth century dragged millions of people out of stable traditional rural cultures and threw them into a situation where the old cultural norms no longer seemed to apply. Nineteenth-century London was a city on the very brink of anarchy; a place where old social structures had collapsed. In many respects such conditions are being paralleled today in the slums of the new cities of the Third

World. Under such extreme conditions, old beliefs were challenged and jettisoned. The new cities were a rich breeding ground for new beliefs and ideologies (notably Marxism).

In addition to the massive changes in social structures brought about by urbanization, there has been a dramatic increase in mobility. A couple of generations ago most people in Britain were probably born, brought up, lived their lives and were buried in the same community. Urbanization and mass transport have put an end to that. We now have an unprecedented degree of contact with other people, including people from other cultures. It has been said that the average Londoner now meets more people in a week than his or her pre-industrial ancestor might have met in a lifetime! In my own case that contact with other cultures included an ex-Muslim from whom I first heard the Christian gospel (and I have British acquaintances who first encountered Christianity in India and Africa).

A special case of that new mobility is the modern phenomenon of mass migrations. Arguably, there has been nothing like it since the *Völkerwanderung* during the last days of the Roman Empire. Modern warfare, persecution, environmental disaster and economic pressures have resulted in the relocation of entire cultures.

Another novel factor in the equation of pluralization is the advent of the mass media of communication. The telephone and computer have shrunk the public world. It has become a 'global village'. Remote spots are now no more than a phone call away.

This was highlighted for me by a recent conversation with a friend who works for a multinational corporation. A regular part of his schedule is a weekly conference with his colleagues. But, since they are scattered across three continents, this conference takes place by live video link. When I was a child this was the stuff of science fiction stories!

This dramatic compression of our temporal and spatial horizons means that it is increasingly difficult to avoid meeting people whose understandings of the world differ radically from our own. Modern businessmen and women, while working in a thoroughly modern context (with its homogenizing effect on culture), have, nevertheless, to co-operate with Muslims or Buddhists or Hindus or Christians or New Agers.

At the private level, the effect of the mass media has been even more dramatic. Thanks to radio and television we now have an open door from the privacy of our own homes into a bewildering variety of belief worlds. In the UK, this has been mitigated to some extent by the BBC and IBA. But deregulation of the airwaves and the advent of cable and satellite broadcasting promises the opening of a veritable Pandora's Box of alternative world-views. If you have ever sampled North American television, you will know what I mean. For example, sampling the available programmes one Sunday afternoon in Toronto, I managed to find a remarkable variety of religious broadcasts (ranging from Roman Catholic and Christian fundamentalist to New Age and Hindu) in addition to the usual crop of sports and old feature films. One Christian commentator on the media asserts that television is the medium *par excellence* of pluralism: 'An avalanche of viewpoints, perspectives, theories, experiences, items of information, is threatening to overwhelm us as individuals and as a society, and to obliterate any real sense of coherence and meaning.' And he asks 'How are we to hold onto, or regain, a sense of the wholeness of God's claim upon our lives in a world that seems fragmented to the point of absurdity?' (Russell-Jones 1992, 1).

PLURALITY AND FRAGMENTATION

The myth of neutrality

The recognition of this plurality is, arguably, one important factor behind the reluctance of the media (particularly public-service television) to interpret what they report. Economic and political analysis is rife, but there is usually no attempt to relate their analyses of events to a single consistent world-view. To do so would be to impose a perspective on their viewers. The words 'propaganda' and 'indoctrination' come to mind. Most TV producers would want to avoid being labelled in this way.

The result is the juxtaposition of contradictory images and assertions. If a controversial event occurs, every conceivable point of view is aired, with the result that they cancel each other out. If what is said is devalued in this way, listeners come to rely more and more on the image projected by the media personalities. Ronald Reagan may not have been particularly adept at putting together a rational argument, but he was a media success because of his mastery of the art of projecting the image of a trustworthy representative of the American dream.

It is not just political events which are treated in this way. There is a similar lack of an interpretative framework to guide viewers through the maze of documentaries. Instead, we are presented with an avalanche of experiences, opinions, theories, speculation and images. It is not at all unusual to find, on the same channel, documentaries taking appreciative, neutral and sceptical stances on the same subject. Controversial scientific theories are often treated in this way, as are contemporary religious beliefs. This was epitomized by Channel 4 in its scheduling side by side of a science documentary (which took for granted that scientific facts are reality) with a series on postmodernism (which called into question the basic assumptions of the preceding programme).

It might be argued that such diversity is a good thing. After all it presents people with all (or many of) the alternatives. Thus they are enabled to think for themselves. This might be more convincing if representatives of the various perspectives were permitted to lay their arguments before the viewing public. In reality, the image has come to dominate over the argument to such an extent that any argument which cannot be presented in a two-minute soundbite (preferably with an appropriate illustration) is ruthlessly edited. Instead of arguments, we tend to be presented with slogans and images.

The ideology of neutrality and a fascination with the sheer brilliance of our technological capacity to handle images are two major factors in this development. However, there is another factor, alluded to in an earlier chapter, which also comes into play. The media are driven not by a desire to be objective and fair, but by commercial considerations. On the one hand, the majority of viewers demand entertainment rather than education, reinforcing the emphasis on images at the expense of arguments. On the other hand, advertisers and sponsors want a milieu which will encourage consumerism. Thus we are more likely to have programmes which review the latest cars and tell us which are the best buys than programmes questioning the necessity of car ownership and offering advice on how to make the best use of public transport. By encouraging consumerism the media are reinforcing the privatization and individualism which are so characteristic of modernity.

Plurality or fragmentation?

The question is whether the situation now facing Western culture is one of increasing cultural plurality or one of vicious fragmentation. At what point does the increasing diversity of voices welcomed by postmodernity cease to be virtuous?

Alternatively, one might ask questions about just what is motivating this apparent plurality. Is it driven by a genuine belief in the real but limited validity of every human culture? Or has it more to do with a cultural malaise which casts doubts upon the meaning and value of all voices?

I suggest that we are living not in a culture which affirms plurality, but in one which is plagued by fragmentation. The rampant privatization and individualism which characterize modernity and which are reinforced by the media are two important roots which feed this fragmentation.

But how has this fragmentation come about? After all, it is not immediately obvious that pluralization must lead to social, cultural or personal fragmentation. I believe the answer lies in its co-ordination with the peculiarly modern phenomenon of a sharp public–private dichotomy.

As we have already seen, the impersonality of the public sphere as it is understood by modernity leads to an emigration inwards; to the privatization of the personal life, of religion, of ethics, of aesthetics, etc. This implies an evacuation of value from the public sphere: it may be the realm of scientific and economic data, but the scientific data have lost any larger meaning and the economic data have become empty symbols. At the same time the individualism of our culture and its ideology of intimacy conspire to elevate the private above the public.

But, thanks to the pragmatic relativism of modernity, the private sphere is widely regarded as the domain of merely relative truths. When explosive pluralization occurs (as it has done in the private sphere during the twentieth century) this now confronts the isolated individual with a bewildering variety of faith options. In such circumstances faith becomes self-conscious and the individual becomes conversion-prone. With individuals much more open to the possibility of changing world-views, we move beyond mere pluralization (the multiplication of more or less stable faith communities) to a state of fragmentation (where the membership of faith communities is continually changing as individuals drift from one to another; where even within one family there may no longer be a shared world-view; where individuals may be unable to maintain their commitment to any one belief system).

The effects of fragmentation

One way of highlighting the difference between a stable cultural plurality and a situation of fragmentation is to explore the effects of the latter.

One effect of fragmentation is the loss of any coherent sense of temporal succession. With respect to the future, this renders its victims incapable of envisaging alternative futures (Harvey 1990, 53–4). Without such a vision of the future, hope ceases to be a meaningful concept. As a corollary of this one would expect to see a resurgence of fatalism and ahistorical mysticism. In relation to the past, fragmentation results in an inability to relate constructively to the tradition. Instead of being rooted in tradition, fragmentation means that all we can do is mine the past for any fragments of tradition which may be presently useful.

THE ABOLITION OF THE PERSON

That last point suggests that fragmentation is not just a social phenomenon. Because human beings are inescapably social animals, social phenomena must have an impact on the individual.

Addiction to change

It is notorious that people in contemporary Western culture are addicted to change. Those who can afford to do so change their cars, computers and clothes in line with rapidly changing fashions rather than because of any inadequacy in the goods they jettison.

At one level this may be attributed to the success of the consumerist ideology in giving soteriological overtones to the act of consumption: 'Buy this suit and you will be saved from being treated as a second-class citizen; buy that car and achieve a successful sex life.' However, at another level, it may be regarded as the internalization of contemporary fragmentation. Os Guinness suggests that 'we have reached the stage in pluralisation where choice is not just a state of affairs, it is a state of mind. Choice has become a value in itself, even a priority. To be modern is to be addicted to choice and change. Change becomes the very essence of life' (Guinness 1983, 100).

But, if change has become the very essence of personal life, it follows that the very notion of individuality is being radically redefined. Identity entails some degree of continuity over time. Now it seems as if the only continuous factor is the fact that there is no continuity! The person is in danger of becoming a series of events which are related only by the fact that they happen to the same body. And, of course, even that degree of continuity is dubious since our bodies are continually changing. In other words, our addiction to change may carry with it the risk of a loss (or at least destabilization) of personal identity.

The malleable individual

We have already noted that the private sphere is understructured and overvalued. Taken together with the destabilization of identity, this creates individuals who are particularly susceptible to public manipulation. Thus the citizens of late modernity are the perfect targets for advertising and propaganda of all kinds; they are the perfect clients for a multitude of new psychological and spiritual therapies; they are potential converts for a farrago of new (and not so new) religious movements.

The role of the mass media in the development of this situation is particularly interesting. They certainly appear to be a major agent of pluralization: the media barons are highly responsive to consumer demands, and with the increasing sophistication of broadcasting they are able to target many different private worlds with greater and greater accuracy. But, paradoxically, the mass media are also a major agent of consumerism (Harvey 1990, 61). They may target the private sphere, but they are firmly rooted in and at the service of the public world. The mass media serve the interests of mass productions by generating mass markets. Similarly, they serve the interests of political parties (in general rather than in particular – though politicians will always complain that particular channels or papers are biased in favour of another party) by reducing matters of social and economic concern to the level of party slogans. Complex situations for which there are a wide range of possible responses, each with their own positive and negative consequences, are thus reduced to a choice between the broad policies of two or three competing political powers.

The suppression of individuality

What happens to events and situations also happens to individuals. What price individuality if it can only be expressed by the possession of a 'personalized' Filofax along with half a million other individuals? Thus Colin Gunton notes that 'The rampant individualism which is so often and rightly deplored conceals a deeper and parallel process in which the impression of pluralism is merely superficial, the mask worn by the suppression of individuality' (Gunton 1992, 84–5).

This is brought out very clearly by David Harvey in his insightful study of postmodernity. In addition to the explicit adaptation to consumerism, Harvey notes that the characteristic psychopathology of Western culture is undergoing a significant shift: from alienation and paranoia to schizophrenia:

Modernism was very much about the pursuit of better futures, even if perpetual frustration of that aim was conducive to paranoia. But postmodernism typically strips away that possibility by concentrating upon the schizophrenic circumstances induced by fragmentation and all those instabilities (including those of language) that prevent us even picturing coherently, let alone devising strategies to produce, some radically different future.   (Harvey 1990, 53–4)

Alienation and paranoia are possibilities only if one possesses a coherent sense of self. Similarly, hope and visions of future possibilities entail a coherent sense of self and time. But for late (or post-)modernity, past and future merge into present. Thus self-fulfilment is sought through variety and intensity of present experience. Under such circumstances consumption has an orgasmic dimension: the fulfilled life is seen as a literal ecstasy (a 'standing outside' of and, therefore, loss of self) of consumption made possible by our purchasing power.

BABEL OR BABYLON?

The abolition of society?

The only too obvious fragmentation of contemporary Western cultures has raised in many minds the spectre of Babel. As I have already noted, the logical conclusion of ideological relativism is precisely Babel: a multitude of entirely unrelated language games which rule out the possibility of communication between cultures. And, with its ideological suspicion of consensus, this is the ideal of at least some forms of postmodernism. Thus Jeremy Begbie notes that 'In its more extreme forms, postmodernism can be regarded as the ultimate expression of the dis-integration of reality, a non-relational vision of reality' (Begbie 1992, 68–9).

But the effects of this pluralization have spread beyond the rarefied realms of religion and philosophy. Alternative economic systems are springing up in many parts of the West as groups and communities unilaterally declare their independence from the global market economy. Centralized functions such as the imposition of law and order are now being encroached on by private security forces and vigilante groups. For religious and philosophical reasons some groups and individuals are now boycotting the public education systems. Community and citizens' groups are increasingly stepping into the gaps in local government. And, perhaps most dramatic, British Muslims have recently set up a shadow Muslim parliament to give voice to their concerns, which, they feel, are not effectively voiced within the British parliamentary system.

The forces of reaction

It would be very easy to read such signs of pluralization as the symptoms of incipient anarchy. Quite apart from such a reading of cultural trends, the degree of freedom created by such a variegated culture has a well-documented tendency to engender a sense of insecurity and fear in sections of the population. Thus one would expect the freedom and plurality of late modernity to result in calls for a return to a more monolithic situation. These calls may be couched in terms of demands for greater law and order and/or stronger central government. Or they may take a more explicitly xenophobic tone, as they have done in Germany, where large numbers of *Gastarbeiter* and a liberal policy towards immigrants and refugees have led significant numbers of German nationals to feel that their own national identity is under threat.

Obviously such fears play into the hands of the powers which currently dominate (or are seeking to dominate) the public world. Vested interests exploit this fear and insecurity for their own ends. Thus at one level calls for a Fortress Europe policy echo the fears of large numbers of European citizens, but at another level they play into the hands of the forces of centralism and domination. That there is something fundamentally wrong about this pressure for unity is clear from the tendency to foster unity by means of scapegoating.

In sharp contrast to the biblical portrayal of Babel stands the historical reality of Babylon: a powerful totalitarian state founded upon a myth of redemptive violence. That such totalitarian possibilities lie uncomfortably close to the surface of at least some sections of Western culture is clear from the recent history of Germany. How many people anticipated that the plurality and libertinism of Weimar Germany would evolve into the totalitarianism of the Nazi era?

But given the choice between fragmentation (with its cargo of anxiety brought about by a lack of any firm foundations) and totalitarianism (which at least makes the trains run on time and tells you very clearly where you belong), many people will opt for the latter. The dysfunctional society is, for many of us, preferable to no society at all (just as, for many abused wives and children, the dysfunctional family is preferable to loneliness). Thus the end of modernity may not be heralded by the discordant whimper so confidently predicted in some quarters. It may instead be trumpeted by the superficially harmonious military music of a new empire.

CHAPTER 10

From Autonomy to Interdependence

INTRODUCTION

This chapter is concerned with a cluster of concepts and beliefs closely associated with modernity and, in particular, classical science. For many people today the outlook generated by these concepts and beliefs is symbolized by the work of Descartes and Newton.

The beliefs in question have already been explored in some detail in earlier chapters. They include the characteristically modern elevation of the scientific method and technical reason, with their emphasis on analysis and reduction. The world-view generated as modern science applied its technical reason in the tradition of Descartes and Newton was that of a mechanistic cosmos: a universe of passive billiard-ball atoms possessing only momentum acted upon by external forces. And, to the extent that the forces and momenta were quantifiable, this cosmos was deterministic. This model of the physical universe was extended to human society, resulting in a mechanistic model of society as an agglomeration of private individuals acted upon by socio-economic forces. Intimations of this may be seen in classical economics or in the behaviourist school of psychology.

This perception of the world as a great machine which is best understood by analysis into its component parts has dominated Western thought for the best part of two centuries. However, in the past half-century it has come increasingly under attack from a variety of quarters.

VOICES OF DISSENT

The new physics

One particularly important source of doubts about the mechanistic cosmos is the very community from which the mechanistic model emerged.

Various observations at the end of the nineteenth century paved the way for physicists to realize that, far from being relatively uninteresting billiard balls, atoms contained within themselves an entire realm of fascinating new phenomena. Investigations of atomic structure rapidly uncovered a sub-atomic world in which many of the old certainties of classical physics simply broke down. In this realm the clear distinction between passive matter and active forces was no longer clear; the simple determinism of Newtonian physics was starved of the necessary data. Perhaps most puzzling of all, at sub-atomic levels the comfortable distinction between observer and observed becomes problematic. Thus one of the continuing debates in this field concerns the extent to which the act of observation affects what is being observed. One physicist and commentator on cultural trends notes that

> The universe is seen as a dynamic web of interrelated events. None of the properties of any part of this web is fundamental; they all follow from the properties of the other parts, and the overall consistency of their interrelations determines the structure of the entire web.   (Capra 1982, 84)

Another aspect of the change in physicists' understanding of the cosmos has been the emergence of various anthropic principles. One of the foundations of classical science was the Copernican revolution in astronomy: the radical shift in perspective which displaced the earth from the centre of the cosmos and enabled

Kepler and others to reinterpret planetary motions in a way which later afforded powerful ammunition to the Newtonian world-view. This displacement of humankind from the centre of things became almost a dogma of classical science, with humankind reduced to the status of ghosts in the world machine (at best, passive spectators who are able to understand but not affect the world process).

Today such a view of humankind's relationship with the cosmos has been undermined by observations which reveal a complex network of strange coincidences in the structure of the cosmos; specifically, coincidences which make it possible for our cosmos to support human life. In order to explain them, astronomers have invoked various forms of what has been called the anthropic principle. In its weak form this is merely the recognition that our existence constitutes a kind of selection effect: if the cosmos did not have this structure, we would not be here to observe it. However, other physicists have argued that our very existence has a significant impact on the cosmos. In a variation of natural theology, yet another school of physical scientists (including Sir Fred Hoyle) has speculated about the existence of a superintelligence 'monkeying with' the structure of the universe to enable our evolution.

A third area in which modern physics is questioning the outlook of its classical forebears is in the development of various kinds of non-equilibrium physics. Newtonian physics simply disregarded phenomena which were highly complex, unstable, non-linear or discontinuous. Modern physicists, by contrast, have taken a particular interest in such phenomena, and new mathematical tools have been developed in order to handle them. The result has been the emergence of the three Cs beloved of recent popularizers of science: catastrophe, chaos and (most recently) complexity theory. Since classical physics dealt with situations which were relatively simple and stable, it greatly reinforced the view that changes were brought about by external forces and that large changes required large forces. Thus, in the face of an impersonal cosmos, the individual human being became an impotent nonentity, incapable of making significant changes. By contrast, the shift of focus to complex unstable systems has highlighted the fact that small changes can have effects out of all proportion to their magnitude. This is symbolized by the contemporary myth of the butterfly: the oft-repeated suggestion that the wing-beat of a butterfly in Surrey might trigger a hurricane on the other side of the world!

Ecology and environmentalism

Another important source of dissent from the older mechanistic view of the world has been the emergence of the science of ecology and the subsequent development of widespread environmental concern. Ecology differs from the classical emphasis on analysis in that the focus of its interest is upon the interrelationships between living organisms. Thus, fundamental to the science of ecology is the concept of an ecosystem: 'an interacting system of plants, animals and micro-organisms together with their physical environment' (Osborn 1993, 12). In other words, the focus is on the system as a whole rather than its component parts.

The most inclusive version of this outlook is that of Jim Lovelock who, in 1979, proposed what has come to be known as the Gaia hypothesis. It is generally agreed that the environment has a profound effect on organisms and their evolution: species must adapt to survive. Lovelock argues that the converse is also true: on a global scale, organisms affect their abiotic environment in such a way as to maintain the environment close to the optimum conditions for the continuation of life. In spite of the connotations of earth mysticism evoked by the rather unfortunate name, Lovelock's version of the hypothesis does appear to be testable, and certainly offers fresh insights into a range of old problems.

Ecology (particularly in its Gaian forms) rests upon an important alternative to the classical tendency to understand systems by reducing them to their components. That may be true of relatively simple systems, but it rapidly ceases to be true as we move to more and more complex systems. Systems thinking becomes essential when we are dealing with complex networks of interrelationships, e.g. in an ecosystem or a social institution.

Even human artifacts such as computer programmes are best understood from a systems perspective. It takes no great skill to write a programme in which each line is syntactically correct. However, ensuring that the programme as a whole is not utter garbage is another matter. Many of the programmes currently in use in offices around the world are so complex (and the possible combinations with other programmes are so varied) that every eventuality simply cannot be covered: new bugs or unexpected forms of behaviour are continually being uncovered by software firms. The programme required to co-ordinate the American Strategic Defence Initiative ('Star Wars') was so complex that it simply could not be tested, and real fears were expressed about what might happen if such a system became operational without testing.

Doubts about modern medicine

A third area which reflects contemporary dissatisfaction with certain aspects of modernity is the widespread criticism of 'conventional' medicine. Western medicine has, of course, evolved in close relationship with Western science. Thus it has come to share the latter's analytical outlook. Fritjof Capra summarizes this outlook as it has been applied to medicine as follows:

> The human body is regarded as a machine that can be analysed in terms of its parts; disease is seen as the malfunctioning of biological mechanisms which are studied from the point of view of cellular and molecular biology; the doctor's role is to intervene, either physically or chemically, to correct the malfunctioning of a specific mechanism.   (Capra 1982, 118)

The result of this outlook has been a technocentric system of health care. Western health-care professionals have been primarily concerned to provide technical solutions to well-defined medical problems. One implication of this outlook has been an ever-increasing reliance on expensive solutions relying upon sophisticated technology. Attempts to export this technology to 'developing' countries have proved disastrous to the countries concerned: a single Western-style hospital may consume a major proportion of such a country's health budget and indenture that country's health system to certain Western suppliers of hospital equipment or medicines.

In the West, concern is increasingly being expressed about the emergence of iatrogenic conditions: illnesses and disorders actually contracted as a by-product of Western medicine itself. Some of these conditions are simply the result of inadequate hygiene or inappropriate environmental conditions (e.g. the proliferation of Legionnaire's disease in some hospital air-conditioning systems). Others are a direct result of medical intervention, e.g. the side-effects of some powerful drugs.

Turning from physical to mental health, questions have been tabled about the social role of psychiatry. To what extent is psychiatry therapeutic? And to what extent is it a form of social control, defining normality and stigmatizing those who fall outside the boundaries of its definition?

More positively, it is increasingly being recognized that health is not simply a matter of narrowly defined physical well-being. For example, it is now generally accepted that some physical disorders are psychosomatic, i.e. caused or worsened by psychological factors. Recent research suggests that psychological factors may even have a direct bearing on the functioning of the body's immune system. Typical of the recent broadening of focus with regard to health would be a World Health Organization definition: 'Health is a state of complete physical, mental and social well-being and not merely the absence of disease or infirmity' (cited by Capra 1982, 119).

As with environmental concern, there is a turning away from a predominantly analytical perspective to a more holistic outlook. It is increasingly felt that Western medicine can no longer afford to concentrate on the body to the exclusion of mind and spirit (and, one might add, society).

TOWARDS A HOLISTIC WORLD-VIEW

The rejection of scientism

As I pointed out in Chapter 2, modernity has been shaped in very significant ways by the scientific project. It would not be an exaggeration to suggest that scientism (the belief that science is capable of giving a complete explanation of reality) is a fundamental (though often unacknowledged) creed of the modern world. However, as I have pointed out, there is growing dissatisfaction with the classical scientific way of explaining things.

This dissatisfaction may be expressed through environmental concern or through a turning towards holistic alternatives to conventional medicine. At a more philosophical level, it may be expressed as a critique of atomism. Or, in relation to persons and society, it may take the form of a rejection of Western individualism.

However, a common factor is that, when challenged to offer a constructive alternative to that which they are questioning, the critics generally point to a more holistic way of looking at the world.

Interconnectedness

Fundamental to a holistic world-view is the principle of the interconnectedness of *all* being. This is a generalization of the basis of scientific ecology rather than a new belief. However, its ultimate origin may be traced back to the Hellenistic doctrine of the Great Chain of Being. This was an elaborate metaphysical schema purporting to show the relationship of all entities to each other and to God. The raw materials for the scheme are to be found in the philosophies of Plato and Aristotle, but it was Neoplatonism which finally organized them into a single coherent system. Augustine's contemporary Macrobius summarizes the doctrine thus:

> Since, from the Supreme God Mind arises, and from Mind, Soul, and since this in turn creates all subsequent things and fills them all with life, and since this single radiance illumines all and is reflected in each, as a single face might be reflected in many mirrors placed in a series; and since all things follow in continuous succession, degenerating in sequence to the very bottom of the series, the attentive observer will discover a connection of parts, from the Supreme God down to the last dregs of things, mutually linked together and without a break. And this is Homer's golden chain, which God, he says, bade hang down from heaven to earth.   (cited by Lovejoy 1936, 63)

Thus all of creation, from the most glorious archangel to the lowliest particle of dust, is envisaged as interrelated in a single hierarchical structure emanating from the One. The extent to which it has penetrated Western thought is clear when we look at how natural the hierarchy still seems to be. We still speak of 'higher' mammals and 'lower' invertebrates. In many religious circles it seems natural to regard purely spiritual beings (angels) as 'higher' than embodied spirits (humans), and those in turn as 'higher' than non-rational animals. Lowest of all is disordered matter, chaos, flux.

Within this metaphysical framework Arthur Lovejoy has identified three key characteristics:

(1) The principle of plenitude: every niche in reality is filled with entities. This implies
(2) Continuity: all gaps will be filled. In the words of Plutarch, 'Nature abhors a vacuum'.

(3)   The principle of gradation: the relationship of entities to one
       another is a hierarchy of perfection with God at the apex.

In Western Christian thought the doctrine of creation succeeded
in breaking the Chain of Being by denying the emanation of all
things from God. But the elaborate hierarchical structure of
creation remained intact. Thus, for example, John Wesley suggests
all three of Lovejoy's principles in the following:

> The whole Progress of Nature is so gradual, that the entire
> Chasm from Plant to Man is filled up with divers Kinds of
> Creatures, rising one above another by so gentle an Ascent
> that the Transitions from one Species to another are almost
> insensible.   (cited by Blackmore and Page 1989, 13)

Like the Great Chain of Being, the modern principle of
interconnectedness relates everything to everything else. All
spiritual and material realities are made mutually interdependent,
but without the hierarchical component of the older doctrine. The
Great Chain has been revived, but it no longer hangs down from
heaven to earth. It has been tied in upon itself in countless ways:
more of a Gordian knot than a chain.

Such a principle allows its adherents to insist that humankind is an
integral part of the natural world. Furthermore, it implies a
rejection of the mind–body dualism which has characterized
modernity: matter and spirit are inextricably bound together.

This new outlook finds expression in a wide variety of holistic
philosophies and therapies. In particular, it has led its adherents to
experiment with traditional alternatives to the modern world-view.
It goes a long way to explaining the recent popularity of ancient
wisdom and primal religions of all kinds. Not surprisingly, this
experimentation also raises fears in the minds of Christian
observers: fears that this reversion to a more holistic way of looking
at the world may be a reversion to pantheism.

From spectators to participants

One of the recurring features in the dissenting voices described
earlier is a significant shift in understanding of how human beings
are related to each other and to the world as a whole. Gone is the
notion that we are essentially passive spectators. The relevance of
the observer to quantum phenomena; the anthropic principles; the
butterfly effect: all point to a new status for human beings as active
and significant participants in the world process.

Such a change of outlook has far-reaching social implications. I have already noted that contemporary reactions against individualism are one expression of a more holistic, more participative perspective: we are no longer isolated individuals but persons who are defined by and define others by our relationships with them. Another implication is that the public–private dichotomy of modernity is called into question. This dichotomy stems in part from the belief that the individual is relatively impotent. However, if social systems are understood as dynamic and unstable rather than deterministic, the actions of individuals take on a new importance. We no longer feel powerless in the face of a mechanistic society.

A less obvious implication is that a more participative outlook will call into question the family structures which have evolved under the impact of modernity. Thus the nuclear family has come in for serious criticism from significant cultural commentators such as Theodore Roszak, who maintains that 'The family as we know it is one of the most damaged and pathetic by-products of industrial upheaval' (Roszak 1981, 159).

Positively, the emergence of a more participative view of human nature should encourage the development of new forms of social participation. Contemporary experimentation with extended families and community lifestyles may well reflect this change. Another form of participation widely reckoned to be of importance for the coming decades is the rapid development of networking. Computer networks, in particular, are a source of both new possibilities and new dangers. It is sometimes said that Singapore is the most networked society in the world. However, that society bears eloquent testimony to the authoritarian potential of networking: the systems now in place in Singapore permit central government an unprecedented knowledge of the activities of its citizens and afford frightening possibilities for social control. On the other hand, the second most networked society in the world is held to be France: a country in which student protests and people power have used the public Minitel system to co-ordinate their activities in a highly effective way. Networks need not mean centralization. Indeed it is now possible to obtain software for computer networks which does not require a central processing unit or bulletin board.

More generally, it is to be hoped that the emergence of this more participative outlook will encourage people to abandon the old acquiescence in the public–private dichotomy. It suggests that we *can* change things. No public institution is so powerful that it can resist those who are determined to bring about real changes. Since the fall of Marxism the writing has been on the wall. No institution commands such complete control of our lives that it is impossible to find uncontrolled gaps. Subversion and cultural change begin by identifying and exploiting those gaps. As Os Guinness pointed out some years before the events in Eastern Europe, the private world of the modern individual is one such gap. When people begin to reconnect their private worlds with the public world, change begins. In the case of what was formerly East Germany, the private world of the churches offered their congregations a relatively safe space in which to explore ideas and even to conceive of the possibility of change in the public world. Out of such uncontrolled gaps grew the movement for the legalization of the New Forum opposition.

The shift from passive spectators to active participants also has implications for our relationship with the natural world. As passive spectators, we were distanced from the natural world. Not being part of nature, it was easy to regard it as no more than a resource from which to extract raw materials for the physical artifacts of culture, and a sink into which to dump our waste products. However, a renewed awareness of our intimate relationship with the natural world holds out the promise of a new way of viewing nature. Instead of a mere resource, it may be seen as our most fundamental environment, our home: most of us do not entertain the possibility of defacing or destroying our homes purely for short-term benefits!

Concluding theological postscript

As I have already noted, the shift towards holism does raise the spectre of pantheism. Calls for a more reverential attitude to nature are often interpreted as calls for a return to nature worship.

There are certainly good grounds for being suspicious of pantheism. In its more monistic forms, it has promoted a devaluing of particularity which can only undermine relatedness. Thus, for example, in some forms of Eastern mysticism the rich variety of the world is dismissed as illusion (the madness of God) and the spiritual path is understood as leading ultimately to the reabsorption of self into the divine unity. The end result might be described as a totalitarianism of the whole.

A satisfactory defence against such an outcome would involve an insistence on the reality and irreducibility of particulars: an insistence on the genuine otherness of the other. This is an essential feature of personal relationships. An I–Thou relationship entails an

'I' and a 'Thou': you and I must be irreducibly different. This insistence on the otherness of the other is closely related to orthodox Christianity's insistence on the transcendence of God: if God is such that a personal relationship with God is possible, then there must be an irreducible difference. Pantheism excludes such possibilities: God cannot have a personal relationship with part of Godself.

CAVEAT EMPTOR

I am conscious that this chapter could be read in an extremely optimistic light. However, I do not want to create that impression. We live at a crucial moment in cultural history. The internal forces generated by both the successes and the failures of modernity are tearing it apart: the vision of the rational society is a dream that is dying. But it is not yet clear what is coming to birth. The emergence of a more holistic perspective is certainly a sign of hope, but it is too early to tell whether the potential promised by such a shift will be fulfilled in reality.

In any case, there continue to be very powerful forces in Western culture militating against the spread of a holistic world-view. For one thing, scientism is by no means dead. The disciples of Monod and Dawkins are quick to portray all things holistic as anti-science or irrational. A couple of years ago I delivered a paper at a conference on the New Age movement in which the chairman began by rubbishing New Agers for wanting to put science back by 300 years. In a similar vein, an article in the *Guardian* (20 April 1990) accuses one leading environmentalist of wanting 'to take us back to the stone age and probably abandon science as we know it'.

A more subtle and certainly more powerful opponent is that of economism. As I pointed out in Chapter 5, modern faith in economics has had a powerful depersonalizing influence on Western culture. By co-opting holistic concepts, it is quite capable of creating the appearance of holism without in any way changing the basic social structures. The phenomenon of New Age consumerism makes this only too clear. Similarly, big business may pay lip service to holism in the latest management training techniques. But those courses generally leave unquestioned the economic and institutional structures within which the managers operate.

CHAPTER 11

From Progress to Paradigm Shifts

THE DEATH OF PROGRESS

The myth of modernity

> The Western story is the myth of progress. This myth, which is
> the implicit religion of Western culture, sees history . . . as a
> story of cumulative development leading up to modern
> Western society.   (Walsh 1992, 15)

The myth of progress is the myth of modernity: the story which
inspires and guides modern men and women. Faith in progress gives
meaning to history and time in that it tells a story of human
perfectibility or, at least, indefinite improvement by means of
technical reason.

The myth of progress informs modernity in both its liberal
capitalist and its Marxist forms. Where they differ is not over
progress, but rather over its mechanism. For liberalism, progress is
gradual and continuous.[1] By contrast, Marxists view progress as
being achieved by revolution or catastrophe.[2] There is a clear
analogue in the debates over evolution, with the liberals corresponding to neo-Darwinian gradualism and the Marxists to the
advocates of punctuated equilibria.[3]

Questioning visible progress

As I pointed out earlier, the modern emphasis on quantifiability is visible in the widespread assumption that progress is empirically observable in human history. However, this assumption was subjected to close and critical scrutiny by John Baillie, who concluded that 'observed progress is mainly technical, whereas believed progress is mainly spiritual' (Baillie 1950, 156). Earlier in his study he summarized what he meant by technical progress thus:

> We have found it principally to consist in an increasing understanding by man of his physical environment, and increasingly successful adjustment to that environment and at the same time a gradually improving technique of control over it; but also, and concomitantly, in advancing social techniques leading to a better adjustment with his human environment.   (Baillie 1950, 37–8)

Four decades later, in the light of what we now know about the extent of modernity's impact on the environment, we might well question the easy assertion that progress is visible in an 'increasingly successful adjustment' to our environment. The intractability of the environmental problems now facing us may well cast doubts upon perceived improvements in our ability to control nature. On a social level, the increasingly visible social problems of modern culture (drug addiction, suicide, violence, the emergence of clear under-classes) call into question assertions about progress in socialization.

In short, if one accepts Baillie's definition of progress,[4] there is little empirical evidence for it in human culture. Of course many people would challenge this assertion. My response to such challenges would be to question their definitions of progress. A neo-classical economist might point to the undoubted increase in the throughput of information in Western culture as evidence of human progress. Scientists and technologists might point to improvements in our problem-solving capacity. I would have to agree with such assertions, but would question whether they say anything about the doctrine of progress, the belief in human perfectibility.

Progress and evil

This empirically unfalsifiable faith in human progress which is characteristic of modernity has come under considerable fire in the twentieth century. One major difficulty for the doctrine is the unprecedented visibility of evil in the contemporary world.

For many people the liberal doctrine of progress foundered in the mud of the battlefields of Flanders. They turned from progress to Nietzsche's doctrine of eternal recurrence. Thus, for example, in 1918 Oswald Spengler's *The Decline of the West* argued that, far from being a tale of human progress, history was a record of the repeated destruction of all cultures and the thwarting of all human aspirations.

Subsequently, the pessimism engendered by the First World War has been reinforced by the Holocaust and Hiroshima. Liberal justifications of evil in terms of a 'vale of soul-making', notions that evil exists as a challenge spurring us on to further progress, do not ring true when heard in the context of Auschwitz or the Holocaust memorial of Yad Vashem. They bear the hallmarks of a doctrine which has evolved for the playing fields of Eton rather than the killing fields of Kampuchea.

Progress and historicism

Another factor which works against faith in progress is the emergence of historicism as part of the Romantic reaction against Enlightenment thought. The doctrine of progress suggests a single end for every human culture, a convergence towards the *telos* of the human race: the global civilization of reason. As I have already pointed out, this was perceived as imperialistic.

Historicism emerged as the historiographical counterpart of Romanticism. It is an alternative to the progressive reading of history which characterizes modernity. For historicism, as for the Romantics in general, each culture and era has its own unique values. This implies that, contrary to Enlightenment belief, there is no global history unified by a concept of progress from less to more civilized. Thus A.L. Rowse could assert that:

> there is of course no *one* rhythm, or *one* plot in history. To
> suppose that there is, or even to expect it and be disappointed,
> is a relic of the religious view of the universe with its
> providential ordering of history to a given *terminus ad
> quem*. (Rowse 1946, 20)

From this perspective, history does not tell a story (certainly not the myth of inevitable progress expected by the fathers of the Enlightenment). Instead, historicists are likely to approach history in a utilitarian manner, seeking within it material which may be of present use. An older form of this was the exemplary approach, e.g.

seeking historical role models for the behaviour of public servants. More commonly today it is treated as a reservoir of human experience into which social scientists may dip in order to test their models.

CAN YOU PARADIGM?

An alternative to the progressive reading of history which has received much attention in recent years is the paradigmatic approach. It has been widely publicized and popularized by spokespersons of the New Age movement.

Paradigms in the history of science

Most advocates of a paradigm approach to culture point back to Thomas Kuhn as the seminal author in this field. Kuhn's *The Structure of Scientific Revolutions* is a rereading of the history of science. In this work, he rejects the traditional notion of gradual cumulative progress in scientific knowledge. It is tempting to suggest that his is a historicist reinterpretation of the history of science in which certain key theories become the characteristic features of competing scientific cultures.

Kuhn offers the following model for theory change in science:

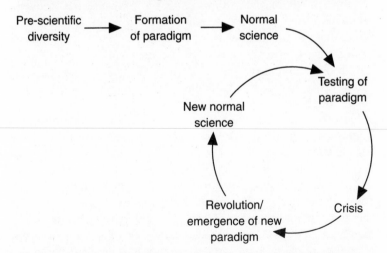

Science begins with the emergence of a paradigm. This is a multivalent term which Kuhn uses in a variety of ways. It may be an exemplary scientific theory which becomes a model for the way in which subsequent generations of scientists work and which provides many of the questions to which they address themselves. More generally it 'stands for the entire constellation of beliefs, values, techniques, and so on shared by the members of a given community' (Kuhn 1970, 175). As such it is largely part of the scientist's tacit knowledge; it is acquired through practising within a particular community and, indeed, may never be explicitly articulated. The paradigm enables members of its community to engage in successful problem-solving and provides criteria for deciding which problems are of interest. Socially, the paradigm creates a sense of community identity by excluding those who adhere to alternative paradigms. Thus it suppresses diversity. In theological terms, the paradigm is the *regula fidei* (rule of faith) of a particular scientific community.

Normal science thus takes place within boundaries set by the paradigm. Scientists operate within traditions: mechanics may be Aristotelian, Newtonian or relativistic; evolution may be Lamarckian or Darwinian. The task of normal science is to explore and articulate the world of the paradigm. Perhaps surprisingly, normal science is *not* concerned with novelty! On the contrary, it tends to ignore mismatches between nature and the paradigm.

Thus a body of anomalies gradually accumulates. Eventually this collection of mismatches may become so large that it can no longer be ignored. Alternatively, some unexpected novelty may throw the community into disarray. A point of crisis is reached. There is increasing dissatisfaction with the current paradigm. Internal disagreements over the meanings of concepts may create disunity within the community. Such periods in the history of science are often clearly marked by a tendency for the scientists facing the crisis to philosophize.

However, dissatisfaction is not a sufficient condition for a scientific revolution to take place. There must be rival candidates for the status of paradigm. Frequently such candidates offer a new way of looking at the subject. Typically they will ignore some of the old problems and raise new problems. Most importantly, a serious contender must have been applied successfully to one (or more) of the outstanding problems facing the old paradigm. In such a situation scientists have to choose between rival paradigms. Kuhn even uses religious language ('conversion') to describe the gestalt shift which must take place. The result is the emergence of a new paradigm and the subsequent suppression of the last vestiges of the old.

Some implications of paradigm theory

This way of looking at change in science has a number of important implications.

First, there are no channels of communication between competing paradigms. Kuhn describes them as incommensurable. A change of paradigm is a change of world-view. The new paradigm brings with it new concerns, new problems and new concepts. Furthermore, terminology which has been transferred from the old paradigm to the new takes on fresh meanings. Thus, for example,

> Chemists could not . . . simply accept Dalton's theory on the evidence, for much of that was still negative. Instead, even after accepting the theory, they still had to beat nature into line . . . When it was done, even the percentage composition of well-known compounds was different. The data themselves had changed. (Kuhn 1970, 135)

Second, it follows from this incommensurability that scientific knowledge is not cumulative. Its content and method are historically (or culturally) conditioned. Thus, while our knowledge of the world may have changed, it has not, on this view, grown.

Third, as befits a historicist reading of science, this approach calls into question whether there has been progress in science. Kuhn's original thesis was sharply criticized on precisely this point. Subsequently Kuhn has expanded his thesis and attempted to show that he is not denying progress. However, his defence of progress involves a redefinition: progress now means improved problem-solving. It is a matter of increased power and is not necessarily related to truth.

Generalizing paradigms

Paradigm theory has been applied to theology (by, e.g., Hans Küng and David Bosch), and to culture as a whole (by, e.g., Fritjof Capra).

Positively, such generalizations highlight the fact that all knowledge is tradition-dependent. They also remind us that traditions can change. As Lesslie Newbigin points out, the possibility of paradigm shifts

> demonstrates that while all exercise of rationality is within a social tradition, the tradition is not ultimate; it is subject to the test of adequacy to the realities which it seeks to grasp. Truth

is grasped, can only be grasped, within a tradition, but traditions can be and are judged adequate or inadequate in respect of their perceived capacity to lead their adherents into the truth.   (Newbigin 1989, 55)

Negatively, paradigm theory reinforces the historicist approach to history. Thus it also reinforces the tendency towards extreme relativism which is so apparent nowadays.

THE EXCLUSIVE PRESENT

The fragmentation of time

Our experience of time as past, present and future gives rise to a perennial philosophical problem: how do we relate these three? But this is not just an abstract theoretical problem. Time is such a fundamental part of our experience of the world that a culture's answer to this question will have a major impact on its character.

For modernity, the doctrine of progress provided the key. Past, present and future were laid out linearly, with (in most versions of the doctrine) the past providing the foundations upon which the present and future could be built. Thus loss of faith in progress could be a major source of despair for modern men and women.

Without progress to connect them, past, present and future become fragmented, atomized. Of course this is not the only factor which has led to the present state of temporal fragmentation. The impact of the visual media, and particularly their portrayal of history, must also be borne in mind: the effect is a video collage in which historical documentaries about Anglo-Saxons may be juxtaposed with Second World War drama and speculative science fiction. Any sense of historical depth is flattened out. Another possible factor is the appearance of digital time-keeping. Robert Banks comments that

Instead of the circular hand movements of the more traditional timepiece, we now have a succession of numbers, together with the preset or hourly 'bleeper'. This has tended to reduce our awareness of the 'flow' of time, and increased our sense of its atomistic, mechanical nature.   (Banks 1983, 103)

One of the clearest signs that a cultural sea change really is taking place is the emergence of a distinctive response to this new experience of time. While modern men and women might despair, *post*modern men and women seem to revel in this fragmentation.

The disappearance of the future

Postmodernity celebrates fragmentation and instability. But, as David Harvey points out, focusing on our schizophrenic circumstances rules out any possibility of developing a coherent picture of a future significantly different from the present (Harvey 1990, 53–4). Thus attention to the future is reduced to the level of projection of or extrapolation from the present. The future is reduced to projects, 'literally things we throw forward, long- or short-term projects, and we measure our progress by the degree of success we have in reaching our self-set targets' (Newbigin 1989, 110).

Forgetting the past

For postmodernity the present is not rooted in the past. It does not follow from the past. Thus history is reduced to an archaeology of ideas (Harvey 1990, 55–6). And in our postmodern excavations of past cultures the integrity which historicism would have allowed them is swept away. We mine the past for useful fragments which can be pasted into present experience. This is dramatically illustrated by the extent to which postmodern artists and architects make use of pastiche or collage. Where an earlier artist might have alluded to or even reworked Rubens's 'Venus at her Toilet', the postmodern artist Rauschenberg merely superimposes a reproduction of it on a surface already covered in other images (including piles of dishes and shop signs). On a more popular level, historical theme parks allow consumers to experience carefully sanitized fragments of the past as entertainment in the present.

The immaculate present

> The new value placed on the transitory, the elusive and the ephemeral, the very celebration of dynamism, discloses a longing for an undefiled, immaculate and stable present.
>
> (Habermas cited by Harvey 1990, 325)

As with most other aspects of culture, it is not possible to isolate a single causal factor (still less a single dominant concept) behind our contemporary concentration on the present.

Harvey highlights radical changes in Western economic practice (as distinct from theory) as one factor in our changing experience of time. Specifically, he argues that during the past two decades the relatively rigid styles of production and marketing characteristic of modernity have been giving way to new, more flexible styles. This increase in flexibility has encouraged the emergence of new sectors of production and new markets. But, most significantly, it has resulted in 'greatly intensified rates of commercial, technological, and organizational innovation' (Harvey 1990, 147), which, in turn, have provoked what Harvey calls time–space compression:

> As space appears to shrink to a 'global village' of telecommunications and a 'spaceship earth' of economic and ecological interdependencies . . . and as time horizons shorten to the point where the present is all there is (the world of the schizophrenic), so we have to learn to cope with an overwhelming sense of *compression* of our spatial and temporal worlds.   (Harvey 1990, 240)

Related to this is the fascination engendered by the visual media. As I have already pointed out, media presentations of historical events are not designed to facilitate critical dialogue with the past. Typically, they take the form of contemporary re-enactment of past events. Thus they re-present history in such a way that historical images are woven into our present experience. Looking at it in a slightly different way, it has been noted that 'Because images are primary and multiple . . . space and time are discontinuous so that, in a sense, neither time nor space exist; both have been dissolved into an eternal present (the present of the image)' (Hebdige cited by Begbie 1992, 67).

The result is an overwhelming immediacy of present experience. The present has an intensity which is orgasmic. The postmodern experience of the ecstatic present is indeed a 'little death': experiencing the present in this way, we die to history and to time. This is equally true of the self-indulgence of the yuppie or the ascetic discipline of the mystic: they are two sides of the same coin, just as amoral libertinism and world-denying asceticism were two sides of the one coin of late Hellenistic gnosticism.

NOTES

1. Of course this does not rule out the possibility of localized regressions. Thus Nazism would tend to be regarded as a regrettable but temporary glitch in the progress of humanity.
2. More precisely, *eu*catastrophe (to use Tolkien's neologism): a happy or beneficial catastrophe.
3. The view that long periods of relative stability are punctuated by brief intervals of explosive evolutionary development.
4. 'a movement in a direction deemed desirable, a change for the better' (Baillie 1950, 2).

PART III

PROCLAIMING GOOD NEWS TODAY

CHAPTER 12

Good News of . . .

GOSPEL

> And there were shepherds living out in the fields near by,
> keeping watch over their flocks at night. An angel of the Lord
> appeared to them, and the glory of the Lord shone around
> them, and they were terrified. But the angel said to them, 'Do
> not be afraid. I bring you good news of great joy that will be
> for all the people.'   (Luke 2.8–10)

The proclamation of good news is a constant theme of the New
Testament: the angelic chorus celebrating Jesus' birth speaks of
good news; Jesus himself proclaims good news; his followers pick up
the theme and spread good news to the corners of the Empire and
beyond.

The term used by the New Testament writers to denote this good
news, *euangelion*, would have been familiar to their first hearers
and readers. In classical Greek the word was used for the reward
given to bearers of good news. It also referred to the good news
itself. Originally this good news would have been the announce-
ment of victory. However, by the time of Christ, its use had been
extended to include other types of good news.

The frequency of its occurrence in the New Testament suggests that it rapidly came to have a specific technical meaning among early Christians. But this technical usage would have remained continuous with its everyday use. Thus Jesus, Paul and the other apostles, in fact every Christian, had good news to share.

The synoptic Gospels present Jesus as proclaiming good news: good news of the kingdom of God. In other words, the good news was of the imminent reign of God on earth. At the same time, it is clear from his words and actions that Jesus regarded himself as the ultimate agent of the kingdom.

Critical studies of the New Testament have often pointed out an important discrepancy between the Gospels and the epistles at this point. In the accounts of Jesus' ministry the good news is of the kingdom; in the other New Testament writings there is a clear shift of emphasis from the kingdom to Jesus himself. Thus Paul can summarize the good news as follows:

> that Christ died for our sins according to the Scriptures, that he was buried, that he was raised on the third day according to the Scriptures, and that he appeared to Peter, and then to the Twelve. After that, he appeared to more than five hundred of the brothers at the same time . . . Then he appeared to James, then to all the apostles, and last of all he appeared to me also.   (1 Cor 15.3b–8a)

References to God's kingdom fade away. And even when the writers refer to good news of God the connection with Jesus is never far away (e.g. Rom 1.1, 9).

Some commentators have interpreted this as a radical change in the nature of the Christian message. Thus Paul is sometimes presented as the creative genius who reworked the message of an itinerant Jewish rabbi to meet the needs of contemporary Hellenistic culture. However, this is to exaggerate a difference of emphasis into a fundamental divergence. Jesus presents himself as the agent of the kingdom. Thus the apostolic proclamation of good news focusing on Jesus points to the one who brings about the reign of God.

The New Testament writers are also clear that this good news is more than mere words. Their message is empowered by God (1 Thess 1.5) or the Holy Spirit (1 Pet 1.12). Thus the message itself commands obedience (2 Thess 1.8) and brings salvation (Rom 1.16).

MANY GOSPELS?

The apparent discrepancy between the gospel preached by Jesus and that of the apostles raises the question of whether there is, in fact, a single coherent Christian message of good news. Many critics of Christianity argue that there is not.

Four Gospels?

The simplest form of this objection is a traditional Islamic response to the Christian Scriptures. Muslims point out that the New Testament contains four Gospels. Thus the Christian message lacks the coherence which would mark it out as a divine message. Our four Gospels can be no more than mere human words about God.

The gospel as doctrine?

There has been a tendency within Western Christianity to concentrate exclusively upon the content of the good news. Thus the gospel has come to be seen as the core of Christian belief; a summary of essential Christian teaching.

On the face of it this seems a safe enough tendency. However, a little knowledge of church history soon reveals that there have been wide divergences over the content of this core. For most of the history of Western Christianity this has not mattered, because the teaching authority of the Western Church has been great enough to suppress the discrepancies. Thus there has been one true gospel and many false gospels.

One unacknowledged effect of this has been to transform the gospel from a simple message of good news into a developed system of doctrine. Thus 'gospel-based' or 'evangelical' have become exclusive designations, referring not so much to the message itself as to subsequent theological interpretations including, e.g., the doctrine of the Trinity.

Differences of opinion over the content of the gospel may not have mattered in the past. But in our anti-authoritarian age it is no longer possible to suppress such differences simply by declaring them heretical. Thus today, if we attempt to identify the gospel with Christian doctrine, we create the impression that there is a plurality of gospels.

A sophisticated example of such pluralism would be the theology of Paul Tillich. For Tillich the gospel, the good news, is the Christian response to the human condition. Fundamental to his theological method is an insistence that we must begin with the most deep-seated human concerns. The good news is the divine answer to the human question. But, since our ultimate concerns are conditioned by history and culture, the content of the good news must change from age to age.

Thus he suggests that the early Christians shared the Hellenistic concern about death and decay. In the light of those anxieties, the gospel message was a promise of immortality or divinization. Following Tertullian and Augustine, the focus of concern in the West shifted from death to guilt. By the Middle Ages (and even more sharply after the Reformation), the main concern of Western Europeans was sin and guilt. And the gospel answer was justification. Tillich goes on to argue that the concepts of guilt and justification are alien to contemporary Western culture. Drawing on existential philosophy, he suggests that our main concern today is estrangement: we live in an impersonal machine-dominated public world, a world in which we are estranged from God, from other races and classes, from family and friends, even from ourselves. Once again the gospel undergoes a transformation to proclaim a message of wholeness through the New Being in Christ. Different gospels for different situations.

An ugly ditch?

The emergence of a strong sense of historical change within Western culture has given rise to another problem for the notion of a unified gospel. For more than two centuries biblical scholars have been acutely aware of the gulf between the historical contexts of the biblical authors and our own situation.

That difference raises the question whether we can ever really know what the gospel meant to Jesus or Paul or James or any of the early Christians. We simply are not part of their culture, and our knowledge of their culture is fragmentary and, in any case, overlaid with centuries of Christian interpretation and reinterpretation. As the literary critic Gabriel Josipovici points out, even relatively uncontentious biblical phrases present the translator with massive problems:

> How, for example, are we to translate the phrase which forms the climax to the episode in which Elijah hears the voice of God (1 Kings 19:12)? Is it a 'still small voice' (AV), a 'low murmuring sound' (NEB), the 'soft whisper of a voice' (Good News Bible), or 'the sound of a gentle breeze' (JB)? The

Hebrew, *kol demamah dakah*, means literally 'voice of thin silence'. But what does *that* mean?   (Josipovici 1988, 33)

Josipovici points out that, much of the time, we simply lack the data to know what a particular combination of Hebrew or Greek words would have conveyed to their original audiences.

A common response to this problem has been to emphasize what the gospel means to the listener today. Today this approach is often associated with liberal forms of Christian theology. Ironically, it first emerged among the Pietist forerunners of evangelicalism, with their great stress upon the application of the text to the life of the believer under the guidance of the Holy Spirit.

What such Pietism (or subjectivism) does is to make the believer's experience of God the true root of theology. Once again this leads to a plurality of 'gospels', since there can be, in principle, as many experiences of God as there are believers!

UNITY IN DIVERSITY

In contrast to these claims that Christianity has many gospels, the New Testament asserts that there is only one gospel. Paul, for example, is quite clear on this point:

> I am astonished that you are so quickly deserting the one who called you by the grace of Christ and are turning to a different gospel – which is really no gospel at all. Evidently some people are throwing you into confusion and are trying to pervert the gospel of Christ. But even if we or an angel from heaven should preach a gospel other than the one we preached to you, let him be eternally condemned! As we have already said, so now I say again: If anybody is preaching to you a gospel other than what you accepted, let him be eternally condemned!
> (Gal 1.6–9)

In spite of the divergence of emphasis between the Gospels and the rest of the New Testament; in spite of the truth in Tillich's point that the gospel addresses itself to the many different ways of expressing human need and concern in different cultures; in spite of the difficulty in bridging the gap between the first century AD (or, for that matter, the sixth century BC) and the twentieth century, there is a single gospel.

Furthermore, this gospel is a specific message. Not all good news is the Christian gospel. Robert Jenson notes that

> There sometimes appears in the institutionalized church a
> strange blend of unbelief and arrogance which, no longer
> having any special thing of its own to say in the world, makes
> up by claiming everyone else's good words as 'really' its
> gospel. What is said in the church may then be a bit of
> sociological analysis, or religious wisdom, of Zen existence-
> jarring, or 'honest encounter' – the possibilities are endless.
> That these words are nevertheless not the gospel does not
> mean that they are not good. There are many things that need
> to be said in the world; if the gospel is true, it is one of them –
> and only one . . . The message of the church is a specific word;
> if the church does not get this word said, all the other words it
> might say are better said by someone else.   (Jenson 1973,
> 3–4)

But what is it that unites the efforts of Christians through the ages
to proclaim the gospel? What relates the message of Paul to that of
Augustine, of Maximus the Confessor, of Simeon the New
Theologian, of Luther, of Calvin, of Jonathan Edwards, of
Kierkegaard, of Henry Venn, of Barth, of Billy Graham?

Consider again Paul's summary of the Christian gospel in 1
Corinthians 15. He does not offer the Corinthians a body of
doctrine or ethics. It is not an abstraction. On the contrary, it is an
outline of a story, a history. As Lesslie Newbigin points out, 'The
content of the gospel is Jesus Christ in the fullness of his ministry,
death and resurrection. The gospel is this and not anything else'
(Newbigin 1989, 153).

Thus the gospel is a retelling of specific events. It is a report that
certain things have happened.

However, events may be reported in different ways. Different
kinds of communication have different effects on their hearers.
Much of the communication between humans has the effect of
binding the hearer to the speaker. It may preclude dialogue
altogether, in which case it poses a master–slave relationship
between speaker and hearer. This is the extreme case of what
usually happens in human communication, namely, that the
speaker seeks to impose obligations upon the hearer, to manipulate
them, to make conditions. Even our promises are often unspoken
attempts at control and manipulation.

It is apparent from the New Testament that the gospel is not a
communication of this kind. It has the form of a promise, but,
unlike human promises, it is unconditional: 'Because Christ has

done this, you may expect that.' In the words of the Reformer Philip Melanchthon, 'The gospel is a promise for the gospel teaches that Christ, the Son of God, has been given for us and is our righteousness before God' (cited by Pelikan 1984, 167). As Jenson notes:

> Only a promise which had death *behind* it could be
> unconditional. Only a promise made about and by one who
> had already died for the sake of his promise, could be
> irreversibly a promise. The narrative content of such a promise
> would be death and resurrection. We are back to 'the
> gospel'.   (Jenson 1973, 8–9)

Because it takes the form of a promise, the gospel holds out the offer of genuine dialogue. Thus it is dipolar: the retelling of the story requires both speakers and hearers; the very act of retelling the story creates a community. It follows that the gospel will always be couched in the language and culture of the recipients. Any communication which requires that the hearers abandon their own language and culture in favour of that of the hearer is imperialistic rather than evangelical.

By the same token, this characteristic means that there is no such thing as the 'pure' gospel. When people speak in such terms, the purity they impose on the gospel entails its divorce from historical, cultural and personal contexts. The gospel becomes an abstraction; a ghost, but an authoritarian one.

In contrast to this ghostly *Diktat*, genuine utterances of the gospel will be as diverse as the rich diversity of human cultures (and, indeed, personalities). The gospel can never be a formula repeated by rote. To be an unconditional promise to specific persons it can never be proclaimed twice in the same way. It is always different, always new . . . and yet always the same!

In the face of such diversity, the only possible basis for unity is a personal one. Again Robert Jenson is helpful:

> In all its changes, the gospel remains itself. But it remains
> *historically* itself, as a person remains himself through the
> changes of his life – or rather, changes precisely in order to
> remain himself, and loses himself if he stops and clings to what
> he was. Indeed, the self-identity of the gospel *is* the self-
> identity of a person: different forms of words are the same
> gospel in that they are all about and in the name of the one,

living and personally self-identical risen Jesus.   (Jenson 1973,
11)

THE HEART OF CHRISTIANITY

What then is the gospel? It is the faithful telling and retelling of
certain historical events (i.e. historical in the sense that we claim
that they occurred in time and space, rather than that they conform
to the canons of modern historiography). In the words of Luther,
'The gospel is a discourse about Christ, that he is the Son of God and
became man for us, that he died and was raised, that he has been
established as Lord over all things' (cited by Pelikan 1984, 167). Or,
even more simply, 'Christ has died, Christ is risen, Christ will come
again'.

But why is this *good* news? Why is it not merely just another
incredible ancient tale of miraculous events? It is gospel precisely
because it is unconditional promise. The assertion is that *this* story is
the key to the meaning of human existence – and not just human
existence; it is the answer to the question of the meaning of life, the
universe and everything. Or, as Lesslie Newbigin puts it, 'the gospel
is to be understood as the clue to history, to universal history and
therefore to the history of each person' (Newbigin 1989, 128).

The proclamation of the gospel as universal and therefore
personal history evokes a crisis. Such an assertion leads to a
radically new situation. In the face of such a claim all our old
mythologies become untenable. It calls for a decision: either Christ
is the clue to history or we must seek some other clue. But a clue
must now be sought (Newbigin 1989, 126).

Christian conversion is the recognition that the history of Jesus *is*
destiny-clueing; that *this* story answers my questions and thereby
answers the question of history; further, that in answering my
questions this story evokes a certain response.

This story is the heart of Christianity. Taken seriously, it offers a
basis for Christian theology which is radically different from the
bases of natural systems of thought about deity. If this story is our
starting-point, we may no longer begin our theology with the
arguments of natural theology. On the contrary, the only legitimate
starting-point for Christian theology is to say that God is whatever
raised Jesus from the dead.

Since the gospel is the clue to history, it is also the basis for Christian discourse about creation. In spite of its recent appropriation by physical scientists, 'creation' is strictly a theological concept. It refers not simply to the beginning of nature, but rather to the relationship between that which raised Jesus from the dead and all other being.

And so we might go on. The distinctively Christian character of every aspect of Christian theology may be shown to lie in this foundation.

CHAPTER 13

To Athens
with Love

THE PUBLIC FACE OF THE GOSPEL

Towards the end of the previous chapter I suggested that what
makes the Christian message 'gospel' or 'good news' is that it offers
the clue to the true meaning of the human story. If this is the case,
the privatization and relativization of religion which has taken place
in Western culture over the past three centuries amounts to nothing
less than a radical falsification of that message. However laudable
the original motives behind such tendencies, their acceptance by the
majority of Western Christians has implicitly denied that the
Christian gospel is good news of this kind.

This insistence that the gospel is private opinion rather than
public truth reduces its capacity to give meaning to life to a purely
individual subjective level. Putting it unkindly, the gospel becomes
a religious crutch to which the inadequate cling in an effort to cope
with life. It is a striking feature of nineteenth- and early twentieth-
century atheism that many of its objections against Christianity
were aimed at precisely this point. For Feuerbach (as later for
Freud), the God of liberal Christianity was a mere projection of the
human psyche; for Marx, religion was 'the opiate of the masses', a
form of escape, a way of coping with an unacceptable reality; for
Nietzsche, religion was the herd's way of controlling/coping with

the adventurous, creative, masterful minority. In other words, their protests were not occasioned by the scandal of the gospel, but rather by the scandal of a subjective religious crutch.

In contrast to this privatization and subjectivization of its message, Christianity has traditionally presented the gospel as a universal message. If in the gospel 'the true meaning of the human story has been disclosed . . . it must be shared universally. It cannot be private opinion' (Newbigin 1989, 125). The only reason for believing the gospel is that it is true. But if we believe this, we cannot deny the gospel by keeping it private.

If the gospel is public truth, then it addresses not merely isolated individuals but persons-in-community. Its destiny-clueing message has implications not only for the personal spirituality of the hearers, but for their relationships, their activities, for every aspect of their life in community. Thus the gospel addresses our corporate life as well as our private life; it addresses the public sphere, our social structures and our cultures. And its message to culture will be the same as its message to the person: it holds out God's unconditional promise to every level of human existence. Thus it is a message of hope, of healing, of wholeness, of new life, of transformation, of fulfilment for culture and society as well as for the person.

That the gospel addresses social and cultural life as well as personal life has, with the exception of post-Enlightenment Western Christianity, been the universal teaching of the Christian churches. Thus, for example, Maurice Reckitt once pointed out that

> If you had told any typical Christian thinker in any century
> from the twelfth to the sixteenth that religion had nothing to
> do with economics and that bishops must not intrude in these
> matters upon the deliberations of laymen . . . he would either
> have trembled for your faith or feared for your reason. He
> would have regarded you, in short, as either a heretic or a
> lunatic. (Reckitt 1935, 12)[1]

However, there have been widely differing views over just *how* the gospel addresses culture. The relationship between the gospel and human cultures has been conceived in a variety of different ways.

It may be helpful to classify and assess these different approaches by drawing parallels between the different ways in which the relationship of gospel and culture has been expressed and the different conceptions of the relationship between Jesus Christ's humanity and his divinity. At its simplest, attention to the latter relationship presented the early Church with three major options. They could conceive of Jesus Christ as a (perfect) human being who became the vehicle for divine action (adoptionism); they could conceive of him as a spiritual being who merely took on human appearance (docetism); or they could conceive of him as somehow holding together humanity and divinity (which I shall call incarnationalism). Similarly, it is possible to conceive of God 'adopting' a particular culture through which to convey the good news; or thinking of the gospel as the basis for an alternative to all human cultures; or somehow holding the gospel in creative tension with each culture encountered by Christians.

'CHRISTIANITY IS JEWISH'

The question of the relationship between the gospel and culture rapidly became a major issue for the first Christians. The first hint of the problem appears with Philip's ministry to the Samaritans (Acts 8.4–8). The joyful response of these outsiders to the message of the gospel must have sent a shock wave through a solidly Jewish church. At any event, two of the most senior figures of the Jerusalem church, Peter and John, are rapidly dispatched to Samaria to investigate (Acts 8.14). However, that shock must have paled to insignificance besides Peter's subsequent encounter with Cornelius. Its importance for the early church can be judged by the amount of space devoted to this one incident by the writer of Acts (Acts 10.1 – 11.18). With the conversion of Cornelius, the gospel had effectively jumped entirely out of the sphere of Hellenistic Jewish culture into pagan Gentile culture.

However, Peter's acceptance of Gentile Christians and Paul's fruitful ministry to the Gentiles did not settle the matter. On the contrary, an influential segment of the Church asserted that Christianity was Jewish. Jesus was the Jewish Messiah; he came to fulfil the law, not abolish it. Thus Christianity was the fulfilment of Judaism, and as such should maintain and perfect that culture.

The view that Christianity is inescapably Jewish is loosely analogous to adoptionism. Interestingly, the Ebionites (who emerged from the Jewish lobby within the apostolic church) also maintained an adoptionist Christology. Just as God has chosen a particular man through whom to act, so he has chosen a particular human culture through which to reveal himself. That culture is Jewish, and the kingdom of God will be the fulfilment of Judaism.

Of course, as history records, the Church did not remain Jewish. But this attitude to particular cultures has been a recurring feature of subsequent Christianity. Within decades of dissociating themselves from Judaism, Hellenistic Gentile Christians were engaged in the intellectual effort of adapting Christianity to prevailing Hellenistic philosophies. This effort is typified by Christian gnostics such as Marcion, but is also visible in more subtle forms in the work of many of the second-century apologists, in Clement of Alexandria and, above all, in Origen. Underlying all these efforts is the unspoken assumption that the kingdom of God will be the fulfilment of *this* culture.

Examples of this kind of thinking may be found throughout the history of the Church. As Richard Niebuhr has pointed out, the most influential recent example of this adoptionist approach to culture can be found in the theology of Protestant liberalism. In his reduction of the gospel to the fatherhood of God and the brotherhood of man, Harnack and his fellow Ritschlians are clearly assimilating the gospel to the world-view of every right-thinking nineteenth-century German gentleman.

The strengths of assimilation

One of the great strengths of this approach to the relationship between the gospel and a culture is its powerful affirmation of human culture. Culture Christianity wants to maintain that Jesus Christ affirms and brings to fulfilment the very best in human culture.

As a result, it places great emphasis on Christian mission to culture. It applauds Christian involvement in the arts and sciences, in business and in politics, in every aspect of secular life. This view of the gospel is closely associated with the emergence in the nineteenth century of the so-called social gospel, i.e. the proclamation of a this-worldly kingdom of God as the fulfilment of Western liberalism.

Objections to assimilation

The chief objection to this way of relating gospel and culture must be the inevitable loss of Christian distinctiveness. Niebuhr highlighted this in his memorable comment on the social gospel: 'A God without wrath brought men without sin into a Kingdom without judgement through the ministrations of a Christ without the Cross' (Niebuhr 1959, 193).

Liberal culture Christianity may set out with the recognition that the kingdom has not yet come in its fullness; it may recognize that there is both good and bad in the culture. However, it is hard to maintain any critical distance from the culture if you believe that it is the kingdom of God in embryo. Identifying the gospel with the culture is, in the end, an uncritical form of affirmation which leads inevitably to the Declaration of 93 German Intellectuals (which, for Karl Barth, revealed the ethical poverty of liberal Protestantism in its affirmation of the Kaiser's militarism), or to the later German-Christianity which sought to purge itself of all Jewish elements.

At the same time, the reduction of the gospel to a proclamation that the kingdom will emerge from *this* culture implies the reduction of the good news to a programme or ideology. Too much emphasis on the continuity between this world and the kingdom undermines the gospel's character as unconditional promise. We begin to see ways in which *we* might bring about the kingdom. Gospel gives way to law.

Another serious objection to this approach is its potential for ethnocentrism. As soon as we begin to think of *this* culture as the seed-bed for the kingdom of God, we will tend to sacralize this culture while at the same time demeaning other cultures. Such cultural imperialism is only too evident in the history of Western Christianity, in particular the history of missions. It was not only German Christians who identified the gospel with the fulfilment of their culture. Thus John Philip of the London Missionary Society could comment that

> While our missionaries . . . are everywhere scattering the
> seeds of civilization, social order, happiness, they are, by the
> most unexceptionable means, extending British interests,
> British influence, and the British empire. Wherever the
> missionary places his standard among a savage tribe, their
> prejudices against the colonial government give way.   (cited
> by Bosch 1991, 305)

Similarly, Cardinal Lavigerie could send out his 'White Fathers' with the charge 'We are working for France [as well as for the kingdom of God]' (cited by Bosch 1991, 304). And, as recently as 1958, a South African cabinet minister could commend mission work as 'the most wonderful opportunity for serving God, but also

the most glorious opportunity for serving the fatherland' (cited by
Bosch 1991, 304).

I am not suggesting that missionaries have been the cynical agents
of colonialism. Rather, it is that, having too closely identified the
fatherland with the kingdom of God, they have seen an extension of
colonial influence as tantamount to an extension of the kingdom.

However, such ethnocentrism is not inevitable. Taken in conjunction with certain other presuppositions, it is quite possible for
culture Christianity to become extremely pluralistic. Again, the
analogy with adoptionism is illuminating. Contemporary forms of
adoptionism do not assume that Jesus of Nazareth was God's
exclusive choice. Focusing on his humanity, they point instead to
the possibility of Christ becoming 'incarnate' in many human lives.
Thus, for example, Matthew Fox asks 'Does the fact that the Christ
became incarnate in Jesus exclude the Christ's becoming incarnate
in others – Lao-Tzu or Buddha or Moses or Sarah or Sojourner
Truth or Gandhi or me or you?' and gives the answer 'Just the
opposite is the case' (Fox 1988, 235). Adapting this possibility to the
relationship between gospel and culture, we might say that the
gospel promises fulfilment to every human culture. Thus, whatever
affirms the aspirations of any culture is 'of the gospel'.

'COME YE OUT FROM AMONG THEM'

Assimilation into Jewish culture was a very real possibility for the
first Christians. However, as Acts and the Pauline epistles reveal, it
was firmly ruled out by the Council of Jerusalem, with its rejection
of circumcision as a Christian initiation rite (Acts 15).

If assimilation is out, perhaps the answer is confrontation. There
is more than a hint of such an approach in the pages of the New
Testament. 'Do not love the world or anything in the world. If
anyone loves the world, the love of the Father is not in him' (John
2.15). '[D]on't you know that friendship with the world is hatred
towards God?' (Jas 4.4). It is present when the writer to the
Hebrews presents the faithful as 'aliens and strangers on earth . . .
longing for a better country – a heavenly one' (Heb 11.13b, 16a),
men and women of whom 'the world was not worthy' (Heb 11.38a).
Even Jesus' own words, 'If you belonged to the world, it would love
you as its own. As it is, you do not belong to the world, but I have
chosen you out of the world. That is why the world hates you' (John
15.19), suggest that our relationship with the world will be
confrontational.

It would appear that, in holding out its unconditional promise, the gospel forces a decision between this ultimate and all other ultimates. There is an implied rejection of all authority except that of Jesus Christ. We remain in the world, but we no longer belong to it.

Put another way, the cross of Christ judges all human cultures. Holding out the promise of ultimate fulfilment to culture, the gospel reveals the shabbiness and corruption of even the best of culture. In that searing light, both personal and structural sins are thrown into sharp relief.

Such radicalism implies that the assimilationism of all forms of culture Christianity from the Judaizers onwards is nothing less than a profound alienation from the heart of the gospel. But it also suggests an affinity with another stark contrast: the presentation of Christ as pure spirit unsullied by contact with the polluted material of this world. This docetic view of Christ so stresses his transcendent deity that it loses sight of his humanity. As a result, salvation is understood in purely spiritual terms: we are redeemed *from* the world, from all the dirt and squalor and nasty physicality of this earth.

Such a confrontational approach will present the gospel as a stark alternative to human cultures. It may suggest that, if we build faithfully upon the rock of the gospel, we may achieve a distinctive Christian culture; and that this culture may, in its turn, be the basis on which God will build his kingdom.

By implication, human cultures are not redeemable. When people are converted to Christianity, they are called out of their own sinful human culture into a Christian alternative. Advocates of this view imply that, when the devil showed Jesus all the kingdoms of the world and said 'I will give you all their authority and splendour, for it has been given to me, and I can give it to anyone I want to' (Luke 4:6), he was simply stating the truth. The logic of this position is that all human cultures are, in fact, nothing less than satanic conspiracies.

The confrontational approach was very influential in early Christianity. One of its foremost exponents was the Roman theologian Tertullian. His famous question 'What has Athens to do with Jerusalem?' (*Praescrip.* 7.9) highlights his aversion to the opinions of philosophers and heretics. For Tertullian, human culture was the locus of sin. He regarded its disordered structures as the medium by which original sin is propagated. Thus, for example, he held that pagan traditions practised by midwives invited wicked spirits to take possession of the human soul at birth (*De anima* 40).

In keeping with this negative view of culture and society, he maintained that political life was to be shunned. To be fair, his objection was, in part, due to what he perceived as the impossibility of disentangling public office within the Roman Empire from paganism and idolatry. But his conclusion is sweeping: 'All the powers and dignities of this world are not only alien from God but hostile to him' (*De idololatria* 17). Thus Christians could not even engage in the financial markets or practise as schoolteachers!

Such confrontation towards the secular culture has been characteristic of sectarian Christian movements throughout the history of the Church. There was a fresh flowering of it after the Reformation, with the Anabaptists denouncing the relationship between Church and state advocated by the mainline Reformers. Like Tertullian before them, they regarded society/culture as the locus of sin. Their response was to set up Christian communities as witnesses to the world of what constitutes authentic Christian culture.

A contemporary example of this approach would be the Christian reconstructionism of some conservative evangelicals. They see the Bible as a detailed blueprint for a divinely ordained alternative culture. Thus they read off its pages a unique 'biblical world-view' which they contrast sharply with contemporary secular world-views.

The strength of confrontation

There can be no doubt that the New Testament paints a picture of Christian life which includes an element of confrontation. Those who advocate such an approach do so on the basis of a radical vision of Christ's lordship. He alone is our authority. Authentic holiness means life lived in the light of his calling, rather than in conformity to the norms of the world.

Thus the confrontational approach is a valuable (and at times prophetic) counter to the complacency and worldliness which beset culture Christianity. For those of us in the mainline churches, the witness of such 'sectarians' and radicals is a salutary reminder not to forget our first love.

The shortcomings of confrontation

However, implicit in the above account are a number of potentially serious shortcomings.

To begin with, such confrontation is potentially dualistic. Secular culture is to be rejected in favour of the spiritual counter-culture of this sect. But it is dangerously easy to go on and identify secular culture with love of the world and hence with love of the material world. Thus, once again, the world of matter (secular culture) is opposed to the world of spirit (the kingdom of God, the sphere of influence of this community).

Another danger is implicit in Tertullian's dismissal of philosophy. The temptation is to set revelation and reason in opposition. Indeed, in one of his famous aphorisms, Tertullian did precisely that, saying of the incarnation 'It is certain because it is impossible' (*De carne Christi* 5). A simple, 'commonsense' gospel is extolled in preference to the careful distinctions of a reasoned theology.

Such a 'commonsensical' approach is dangerous precisely because it is terribly easy to be uncritical of one's own presuppositions. 'The Bible clearly says . . .' 'A commonsense interpretation of this passage indicates that . . .' The danger is precisely the same as that of natural theology. What we take to be natural or commonsense because of our cultural context creeps into our theology and our biblical interpretation without our being aware of it.

Ironically, the result of confrontation may be an unacknowledged assimilation of certain aspects of our culture. Thus Christian fundamentalism often looks and sounds much the same as political conservatism. Alternatively, consider the way in which liberation theology manages to wed biblicism to Marxist ideology. Both the liberation theologians and the fundamentalists have fallen into this trap of assuming that the meaning of the biblical texts is obvious.

In fact, of course, many Christians of this school stop short of the kind of simplicity they claim. Tertullian's rejection of philosophy, for example, turns out to be disingenuous, as he invokes not only Stoicism but also Aristotle, Heraclitus and Democritus in his defence of what he takes to be the biblical doctrine of the soul (Pelikan 1971, 50).

The fundamental difficulty with a confrontational approach to culture lies in the fact that it stands in tension with the commission to proclaim the good news to every culture. Christian mission entails a *positive* engagement with the culture.

At the very minimum we must use the language of a specific human culture in order to communicate the gospel. But language and culture are inextricably interconnected. Take, for example, a Christian reconstructionist approach to economics. The claim is sometimes made that we can read a biblical economics from the pages of the Bible. Now, it is certainly true that many aspects of the economic life of various ancient Near Eastern and Hellenistic cultures may be found in the pages of the Bible. But those cultures had no concept of economics as we understand it, nor did they have the vocabulary to express what we understand by 'economics'. In fact, the very word 'economics'

> cannot be translated into Greek or Latin. Neither can the basic terms, such as labor, production, capital, investment, income, circulation, demand, entrepreneur, utility – at least not in the abstract form required for economic analysis.
> (M.I. Finley cited by Fraser and Campolo 1992, 177)

Thus, while it may be possible to piece together the elements of economic life depicted in the Bible to create a variety of economic systems consistent with biblical teaching, it is anachronistic and disingenuous to speak of a biblical economics. When someone proposes a 'biblical economics', it may well be that he or she is attempting to baptize certain aspects of modern Western culture.

Consistent confrontation would undermine Christian mission. Indeed, consistency would demand that we give up even the languages of the cultures to which we have been sent. The language is part of the culture and shares in the shortcomings of the culture. Real 'gospel purity' could only be achieved by the use of a specifically Christian language built entirely upon Christian principles. But, of course, such a sectarian Esperanto would communicate with no one: the very attempt to present the gospel in all its purity would be the ultimate denial of the gospel! This is impossible. But far too many Christians take refuge from the world in a semi-theological jargon which renders their message irrelevant and impotent in the face of other cultural forces.

INCARNATING GOOD NEWS

That Jesus

According to the orthodox doctrine of the incarnation, God became a man. The event of Jesus Christ was not simply a matter of God conferring divinity upon a chosen human being (adoptionism). Nor did God simply take on the appearance of human form (docetism). No, God became a man: deity has been revealed through the life, death and resurrection of a historically identifiable male Jew.

This, of course, is the so-called scandal of particularity. Christian faith is not rooted in a concept or a lofty ideal, but in a specific historical person: Jesus of Nazareth. Like any other human being, he was a product of the personal and social relationships in which he was embedded. He was shaped by his family: he would not be *that* Jesus if it were not for the precise shape of his relationships with Mary and Joseph. He was shaped by his friendships: *that* Jesus was a friend of the couple whose wedding he attended in Cana, *that* Jesus later had a motley bunch of friends including prostitutes and collaborators with the Romans. He was shaped by his childhood teachers: we cannot know what effect the example of the village elders and the local rabbi had on him as he was growing up. And, of course, alongside all of these human relationships, he retained his unique personal relationships with the other persons of the Trinity.

Not only was he part of a specific network of personal and social relationships, he was also part of a specific culture. He was a first-century Jew and he remained faithful to his Jewish heritage. At many points he affirmed the culture in which he lived. Of course there were also many points at which he challenged the culture. For example, his cleansing of the Temple was an attack on the economic structures of Jerusalem. But it had the character of a call to be faithful to the deeper structures of Jewish culture rather than that of an attack upon the culture itself. Thus, although he questioned and criticized contemporary Jewish practice, he never took it to the point of calling into question his own Jewishness. Rather, he maintained a creative tension between his ministry and the culture in which he lived.

A similar relationship should pertain between our proclamation of the gospel and the culture in which we live. Christian mission to human cultures calls for a creative tension (the tension of a genuine dialogue) rather than uncritical affirmation of the culture in its entirety or wholesale judgement of the culture.

Pentecost and culture

Why did the apostles reject the culture Christianity of the Judaizers? Was it perhaps because an incarnational view of the relationship between gospel and culture was implicit in their experience of Pentecost?

Acts 2 locates the origin of the Christian Church and its mission in the events of that feast. Although the resurrection had taken place, the disciples were commanded to contain themselves and to remain in Jerusalem awaiting the gift of the Holy Spirit (Acts 1.4).

When the Holy Spirit finally comes upon them at Pentecost, he constitutes them a new worshipping community. But what marks this worshipping community as different, what amazes outsiders, is the fact that 'we hear them declaring the wonders of God in our own tongues!' (Acts 2.11b). The significance of this event would not be lost on the Jews gathered in Jerusalem for the feast. As Bishop Peter Selby points out, 'those Jews who first heard the story of Pentecost would have been in no doubt that it amounted to a story of God transcending the boundaries established in the aftermath of Babel' (Selby 1991, 18).

However, it was most definitely not a *reversal* of Babel. The Genesis story of Babel portrays the loss of a primordial cultural unity, symbolized by unity of language (Gen 11.1–9). The gift of tongues at Pentecost did not restore that primordial unity. The disciples were united in their worship of God by the Holy Spirit, but their expression of that worship was as diverse as the cultural diversity of their hearers. What has happened is that the gospel has become 'accessible within and despite the boundaries and con-straints which the diversity of human culture and nationality establish' (Selby 1991, 18).

We may take it that the languages referred to in Acts 2.8–11 are representative of *every* language, and hence, of *every* culture. This implies that through the Holy Spirit human beings are enabled to express the gospel and praise God *in every culture*. As Lamin Sanneh points out, 'The "many tongues" of Pentecost affirmed God's acceptance of all cultures within the scheme of salvation, reinforcing the position that Jews and Gentiles were equal before God' (Sanneh 1989, 46).

The unity depicted by Pentecost is not one which depends upon a common culture or racial origins. On the contrary, the people are united by the fact that, under the guidance of the Spirit, the apostles praise God and proclaim good news in every language: the same message, the same God, the same praise, but without any suppression of cultural diversity.

The book of Acts depicts the earliest stages of the Christian mission as it flows out of that Pentecost experience. Gradually the first Christians begin to realize that the Holy Spirit was not limited by their cultural prejudices. As they begin to preach the gospel in response to the call of God, they begin to realize the implications of Pentecost: they are Jews belonging to a community born in the very heart of Judaism, but this community has to be open to Samaritans as Samaritans and to Gentiles as Gentiles. Pentecost has opened the doors to Gentiles in a completely new way, establishing the

Christian community as one which encompasses all cultural diversity.

The gospel in culture

Just as Jesus grew up, exercised his ministry and died in a specific cultural context, so the Bible evolved in specific cultural contexts. The Old Testament crystallized out of the interaction of the ancient Hebrews with the surrounding cultures. The themes of exodus, covenant, exile and restoration all grew out of such interactions. Furthermore, many of the literary forms of the Old Testament are related to similar forms in the literature of the surrounding cultures. Thus, for example, there are affinities between the Old Testament wisdom literature and the wisdom literature of other cultures.

Similarly, the writers of the New Testament wrote from within a specific culture, that of Hellenistic Judaism. They used language and concepts which their readers would have understood. After all, they were attempting to convey a message of good news. As Lesslie Newbigin has pointed out, 'Every attempt by human beings to grasp in human words what God has done in Jesus Christ must necessarily be expressed in terms of the culture of which those human beings are a part' (Newbigin 1991b, 2).

All human words about God are spoken in the context of a specific culture. Thus the gospel must be expressed in forms appropriate to the culture in which it is being proclaimed. This is not merely a matter of words. Beyond finding the right language, proclamation of the gospel and worship of the Christian God will require the discovery of appropriate rituals and symbols. For example, Indian Christians living in Britain are now exploring the Hindu festival of Diwali as a culturally appropriate way for them to worship God.

The gospel to culture

As I have already pointed out, the apostles set themselves against the option of identifying the gospel exclusively with Judaism. Negatively, this was a stand against the sacralization of any human culture. Positively, it implies a commitment to communicate the good news of Jesus Christ in *all* cultures.

This decision has striking implications for Christianity. It sets the heart of the Christian message in stark contrast to the scriptures of other major world religions. Most religions insist that their holy books can only be properly appreciated in the original languages. This is true of Judaism, of Islam, of Hinduism. The tendency to elevate the language (and hence the original culture) of the sacred writings above other languages may even be seen in new religious movements.[2] It results in an approach to the propagation of the religion which has been called mission by diffusion: 'By it religion expands from its initial cultural base and is implanted in other societies primarily as a matter of cultural identity' (Sanneh 1989, 29).

Not so with Christianity. As Lamin Sanneh has ably pointed out, the apostolic decision to communicate with Hellenistic Gentiles in Greek amounted to an assertion of the translatability of the gospel. It meant that Christian mission would be characterized by translation rather than diffusion: 'The other way is to make the recipient culture the true and final locus of the proclamation, so that the religion arrives without the presumption of cultural rejection' (Sanneh 1989, 29).

Thus authentic Christian mission proceeds by translating the gospel into the culture of those with whom we are seeking to communicate. This contrasts sharply with those Christian expressions of cultural imperialism which held that natives had to be indoctrinated in European civilization before they could grasp the gospel.

The translatability of the gospel implies a radical cultural pluralism. It not only recognizes the fact of cultural plurality, but actively celebrates that plurality. This is a bitter pill for us to swallow. Ethnocentrism is very much a part of our fallen human nature. Thus Sanneh points out that

> For most of us it is difficult enough to respect those with whom we might disagree, to say nothing of those who might be different from us in culture, language, and tradition. For all of us pluralism can be a rock of stumbling, but for God it is the cornerstone of the universal design.   (Sanneh 1989, 27)

It means being humble enough to admit of an alien culture that this too is a context in which the gospel can be successfully communicated and God glorified. If the gospel is affirmative of *all* human culture in this way, it means that in our proclamation we must be careful to avoid calling upon converts to abandon their native culture. It is arguable that one of the fundamental weaknesses of the Christian churches of Europe is a tendency to demand that people do not merely acknowledge the lordship of Christ but also abandon their former way of life in favour of that of a peculiar middle-class sub-culture.

The gospel against culture

But if every human culture has its own legitimate place in God's designs, it is also true that every human culture is relativized by being so placed. Pentecost gives the lie to the Enlightenment vision of an ultimate human culture. It also gives the lie to any talk of a unique Christian culture. Christendom may have had its glorious aspects but, in the light of Pentecost, it has to be judged an exercise in cultural idolatry. When the Roman Church absolutized the Latin language and culture, it abandoned Paul and sided with the Judaizers. Any effort to absolutize a particular cultural expression of the gospel (e.g. the efforts of the Prayer Book Society to maintain support for the Church of England's Book of Common Prayer) is similarly an exercise in cultural idolatry.

Human cultures are relativized by having a legitimate place in God's design. 'Having a place' in the purposes of God implies that they are finite. There is no one culture capable of fully expressing the gospel. That is why it must be expressed in every nation, tribe, people and language. Each culture has its own unique contribution to make to the full expression of God's praises. Each culture has its own unique and legitimate insights into the nature of reality, without which our praise of God would be impoverished. Each has its own unique theme to contribute to the cosmic symphony of praise.

But the gospel does not merely relativize cultures. It also proclaims a word of judgement against *every* human culture. Human cultures are not only finite, but also fallen: they are not merely *limited* expressions of being human together, but *actively distorted* expressions of being human together.

Thus the gospel calls upon us to maintain a critical distance from our own culture. As we listen to the good news of God in Christ we must pay particular attention to the points at which it implicitly or explicitly criticizes our own culture. If we respond to biblical passages with embarrassment, offence or incomprehension, that may well indicate that something in those passages is out of harmony with our basic presuppositions. For example, Jesus' parable of the workers in the vineyard (Matt 20.1–16), with its emphasis on equal pay for all regardless of how much work they have done, runs counter to our most basic ideas of economic justice.

The fact that the gospel stands against every culture does not imply that we have *carte blanche* to criticize other cultures. That is a job for Christians who are a part of those cultures. Hence Paul Hiebert adds a fourth self to the traditional three selves of Christian mission: self-theologizing.[3] We cannot presume to do theology for other places and times. To do so is to risk Christ's stricture 'what is that to you? You must follow me' (John 21.22b). Our call is to work out what following Jesus means in our own time and place, in our own culture.

The conversion of culture

Finally, the goal of Christian mission to a culture will be nothing short of conversion of that culture.

This does not mean that all cultures must be reduced to some hypothetical uniform Christian culture. Again, the analogy with personal conversion makes that clear. As I have said before, there is no unique Christian culture, any more than there is a unique model of what it is to be a Christian.

Neither can the conversion of culture mean a reversion to Christendom.

The conversion of culture means allowing the gospel to bring that specific culture to fulfilment. The result will be a family of different cultures, each expressing and reflecting the Christian gospel in its own way. Christendom was one particular culture, expressing (and mis-expressing) Christianity in one particular way. Other cultures need to find their own paths.

The goal is eschatological. Christianity's Pentecostal affirmation of human cultures is not merely a temporary arrangement for the sake of more effective mission. On the contrary, the book of Revelation suggests that ultimately Babel will not be reversed. We have to look forward to a transformation, not a reversal. Those who praise God in the *eschaton* are still identifiably from 'every nation, tribe, people and language' (Rev 7.9). Cultural pluralism is an integral part of God's universal design. If individual Christians may be likened to the individual instruments playing in the eschatological symphony of creation, then the rich variety of human cultures correspond to different sections of the orchestra. No two cultures will glorify God in precisely the same way: but every one is essential if the symphony is to be complete.

NOTES

1. In fact it was only in the nineteenth century that economics was divorced from its original context as a branch of moral philosophy.
2. For example, serious students of anthroposophy study the works of Rudolf Steiner in the original German.
3. The three selves enunciated by Rufus Anderson and Henry Venn were self-propagation, self-support and self-governance. These were to be the goals of all missionary work on behalf of a recipient church.

CHAPTER 14

Good News for the Church

BEGINNING WITH THE CHURCH

Talk of relating the gospel to human culture inevitably raises questions about the role of the Church and its relationship to the gospel.

Christian churches have regularly claimed intellectual property rights over the gospel. The Church shaped and mediated the gospel by creating the canon of Scripture. The Church is the kingdom towards which the gospel points. At times talk of communicating the gospel has been identified with extending the influence of the Church.

One of the most important insights of the Reformation was that, contrary to such tendencies, the good news of Jesus Christ is not determined in any way by the Church. The role of the Church in selecting those books which now form the canon of sacred Scripture and in interpreting their contents is in no way determinative of the gospel: it remains the gospel of Christ, not the gospel of the Church.

Instead, the Reformers saw the Church as the creature of the Word (Schwöbel 1989). In other words, the gospel is constitutive of the Church. The Church happens as people gather together in response to the communication of the good news of Jesus Christ. Thus the primary reality of the Church is not institutional. Rather, it is the event of listening and responding to the gospel as a community. The event is holy to the extent that the community of listeners responds faithfully to the good news; it is catholic to the extent that the good news is communicated in many different languages and cultures; it is apostolic to the extent that the good news to which we respond is the same as that which inspired the apostles.

Of course, as Christians gather together in response to the gospel they will organize themselves. If the Church is to be a social reality, it must have institutional structures. However, the New Testament has little to say about such structures. Various ministries and leadership roles are mentioned, but they are never clearly defined, and the lists even appear to conflict with one another. Lacking clear scriptural guidelines, Christian forms of organization will inevitably reflect to some extent the social structures which are possible within a specific culture.[1]

Thus the male-dominated hierarchical forms of ministry which are still prevalent in the older churches are, in part, a reflection of early Christianity's adaptation to the social structures of imperial Rome. As churches adapt to the social structures of modernity, there is an increasing emphasis on bureaucracy and management by committee. This is particularly noticeable in some of the new American churches and in para-church organizations such as the World Council of Churches.

Thus Christians inevitably meet the culture within the Church. More precisely, the Christian churches constitute distinctive sub-cultures shaped to varying degrees by the gospel, the surrounding culture and the culture of their founding fathers. It follows from this that the first dialogue which must be established is that between the gospel and the various things which we call church in our culture.

THE CHURCH AS PUBLIC LIE

Failure to engage in that fundamental dialogue leads again and again to the phenomenon which some participants at an inter-national consultation on 'The Gospel as Public Truth' described as 'the Church as public lie'. Too often we find that the life of the Church contradicts the message which ought to be constitutive of its very existence. I am not referring here to the moral or other failings of individual Christians, but to the institutional compromises which quite illegitimately ease the tension between the Church and its cultural context. The Church is called to be a community of resident aliens but finds it more comfortable to be either wholehearted residents or equally wholehearted aliens!

Constantinianism

The conversion to Christianity of the Roman emperor Constantine presented the early Church with both its greatest opportunity to influence the culture of the Empire and its greatest challenge. Failure to rise to that challenge led to the besetting sin of the pre-modern Church: its identification with the political powers.

What happened was that the Church adapted only too well to the imperial power structures. Aspects of Christian teaching which did not sit well with this adaptation were rapidly suppressed instead of being permitted to function as a critique of the culture. Thus the Church failed in its transformative role. For example, the earlier Christian identification of Rome with Babylon (an identification which amounted to a radical critique of Roman domination) was conveniently overlooked.

By providing fresh religious legitimation for the political status quo, the post-Constantinian Church thus effectively betrayed Christ, who was crucified by those same power structures. The followers of one whose kingdom was not of this world readily identified that kingdom with the all too worldly Empire.

There followed an inevitable subversion of the missionary nature of the Church. As the remnants of the Roman Empire gradually evolved into Christendom, mission came to be identified with imperial expansion. Conversion came to mean the imposition of a Christian ruling class upon a people and the submission of that ruling class to the spiritual (and temporal) authority of the Pope. It was in such a context that the crusades were born.[2] The imperialism which has accompanied much of the subsequent missionary activity of Western Christianity may be seen as a hangover from this identification.

The individualistic Church

The religious and political strife which eventually brought Christendom to an end left the Church in an entirely new situation. However, the tradition of cosy assimilation to the prevailing culture continued.

Syncretism with modernity has resulted in a Church which looks very different from the imperialistic Church of Christendom. The modern Church faithfully reflects modern culture.

In particular, it accepts without question the privatization of religion. This has resulted in a radical depoliticization of many churches. Many of the institutions to which we now give that name would not be recognized as churches by the earliest Christians. As Lesslie Newbigin has pointed out, the early Church 'did not regard itself as a society for the promotion of the personal salvation of its members . . . It was the public assembly to which all humankind was summoned, which was called not by the town clerk but by God' (Newbigin 1983, 33). By contrast, one wit at an early conference of The Gospel and Our Culture commented that 'Jesus called us to be fishers of men. We train our ministers to be aquarium keepers.' The public dimension of the Church has been largely lost. As a consequence the churches have by and large failed to provide adequate support for the political initiatives of Christian lay people. Thus, for example, British socialism, which had its historical roots in popular Christianity, has become a predominantly secular movement and many of its supporters have been alienated by the institutional churches.

This privatization has resulted in the emergence of a ghetto Christianity in which the Church is treated as one sub-culture within modernity. It has its own private language, and this reinforces the notion that it is an exclusive religious club for those whose hobby is a particular kind of spirituality. Seen in this light, the depoliticization of Christianity is quite reasonable: the office-bearers of a religious club have no more call to speak out about government policy than, say, the office-bearers of a train-spotting society! The martyrs of the early Church died precisely because they refused to accept such privatization.

Closely related to this privatization is the individualism of which we have already spoken.

In February 1989 the General Synod of the Church of England rejected proposals which would have ensured that a larger number of members of minority ethnic groups were enabled to take part in the government of the Church at the highest level. After the decision the official comment was 'This is not a matter of racism'. And, indeed, during the debate speakers on both sides agreed that there should be no question of ethnic distinction within the Christian Church. Reflecting on this decision, the former Bishop of Kingston, Peter Selby, comments that

> We are thus invited to believe that membership in the Body of Christ does not so much include or transcend our ethnic and

other differences as obliterate them. Our Christian
membership is as discrete individuals, cut off from the cultural
roots and social background which might have made us what
we are and which might constitute a significant part of what we
have to offer to one another. All sorts of gifts can accompany
us into the Church, but not those that come with our ethnic
origin. (Selby 1991, 9)

This suggests that individualism has become a form of fetishism
for the modern Church. Like the fetishism of commodities, the
fetishism of the individual draws a convenient veil over the
unpleasant reality of inequality and injustice. By focusing exclusively on the private individual the modern institutional Church
suppresses real social and cultural differences and thus hides any
inequalities which continue within the Church.

Peter Selby's comments highlight the covert racism within the
institutional Church, even among those who would pride themselves on their liberalism. Similar comments might have been made
about the continuing sexism of many churches. I am thinking now,
not of those churches which refuse to admit women to their
ministry, but specifically of those which do. Churches such as the
main Episcopal churches of North America and the Presbyterian
Church of Scotland recognize that women may fully exercise a
Christian ministry. However, in practice, women tend to be forced
into those situations that no man would accept – the more
influential and more affluent congregations tend to remain male
preserves. Similarly, the training of women for ministry tends to be
carried on in a context which was designed by men and adapted for
the needs of men.

THE CHURCH AS SURPRISE

Missiology . . . is the study of the Church as surprise.   (Ivan
Illich cited by Bosch 1979, 59)

The good news is that our faithlessness does not ultimately
compromise the gospel. God is not limited by the Church. And,
since the mission is God's rather than the Church's, it goes on in
spite of the sexism, racism and imperialism of particular expressions
of Christianity. The history of Christian missions is a story of one
surprise after another as authentic Christianity takes on new forms
in different cultures, often in spite of the missionaries.

Thus, for example, Christianity has taken root and grown into many new and exotic plants in the soil of Africa. The missionaries may have gone to Africa believing that they must convert the natives to European civilization before they could be open to the gospel. But, as Lamin Sanneh has pointed out, the very act of translating the Bible into many new languages and dialects led directly to the nurturing of African nationalism. The gospel may have been taken to Africa as a tool of European imperialism, but it was received by many as a message of genuine liberation. The vitality of Christianity in that continent is clearly visible in the rich diversity of independent churches which have grown up with their own theologies.[3]

The mother of the Church

The Christian gospel is good news first of all for all organizations that call themselves churches. The good news is that being Church is *not* our responsibility. The Holy Spirit is the life-giver, the mother who gives birth to the Church by enabling people to respond to the gospel. As I said earlier, Church happens when people come together in response to the gospel. The good news is that we are relieved even of the burden of ensuring that coming together happens. The One who brings people together to be Church is the Holy Spirit.

Of course this means that Church may happen in many different ways, not all of them authorized by some human institution. It may happen in the meeting of a house group or a Mothers' Union, in a gathering of Franciscan tertiaries or charismatic evangelicals. I know of a group of people on the margins of the Church of England who have come together as a mutual support group: what goes on in their gatherings is often more truly Church than many of the parish churches to which they belong. There is a church which meets regularly in a London pub. In Sheffield, the Nine O'clock Service has recently outgrown a large Anglican church building in which it was founded, and in which its activities included something that can only be described as a Christian night club.

The Holy Spirit as the mother of the Church breathes into it an openness to the future which is in marked contrast to the conformity to the past more typical of human institutions. The life-giver is the giver of novelty who enables us to take risks, who gives us the courage to follow Jesus 'outside the camp, bearing the disgrace he bore' (Heb 13.13), to become resident aliens who refuse simply to identify with existing power structures, because of our vision of a heavenly city.

Ite missa est

If Church is the event of people coming together in response to the good news of Jesus, it is also the event of those same people being sent out to carry that good news to others and invite them to the gathering. Thus mission and Church are inseparable. Christian mission which does not envisage church-planting, and churches which do not envisage engaging in mission, are equally contradictions in terms. As one of the leading missiologists of our generation put it, 'the church's being called out of the world sends her into the world; her being sent into the world calls her out of the world' (Bosch 1979, 15). Or consider the following prayer from the Alternative Service Book:

> Almighty God,
> We thank you for feeding us
> with the body and blood of your Son Jesus Christ.
> Through him we offer you our souls and bodies
> to be a living sacrifice.
> Send us out in the power of your Spirit
> to live and work
> to your praise and glory.

Faithfulness to that vocation has again and again led to un-co-ordinated lay missionary activity. It has often been resisted by institutional churches or manipulated by imperial interests, but through that activity Christianity has become a truly global religion. It has proved capable of being transplanted into every human culture. Furthermore, it has produced in the last century a dramatic shift in the centre of gravity of the Church. This is often overlooked by European and North American Christians who are used to assessing organizations in terms of economic power. Because of our acquiescence in the power structures of modernity we share in its global economic influence. But the spiritual heart of Christianity now lies elsewhere, with the vital churches of Africa, Asia and Latin America. Perhaps for Western Christians with their Eurocentric (or US-centric) bias this is the biggest surprise of all in the Church as surprise.

NOTES

1. This is precisely what you would expect in a religion whose attitude to mission was that described in the previous chapter.
2. From the point of view of revealing the true purpose of the crusades, some of the most significant were those against heretics and other Christians who did not acknowledge the authority of Rome, e.g. the Albigensian crusade, the sack of Constantinople and the campaigns of the Teutonic Knights against the Orthodox Rus.
3. Similar responses have been forthcoming among oppressed peoples in many other situations, from the Black spirituality of North America to the Minjung theology of Korea. Christianity may come as the religion of the masters, but its native soil is in the experience of the enslaved.

CHAPTER 15

Principalities and Powers

BEYOND MATERIALISM

One of the characteristic assumptions of modernity was materialism. For modern men and women, explanations in terms of matter
and efficient causes were regarded as entirely adequate. Assertions
of belief in spiritual realities (such as God, but, even more so,
angels, demons, fairies etc.) were met with blank incomprehension
or embarrassed silence. Such admissions marked one out as 'pre-
modern', 'pre-critical', or even 'superstitious'.

However, materialism no longer has the attraction it once had.
An increasing chorus of dissenting voices from a variety of quarters
calls us to look beyond materialism.

One such quarter is psychoanalysis. Certain schools, notably
Jungian analysis and transpersonal psychology, ascribe a degree of
reality to psychological phenomena which would be anathema to
any materialist. Indeed, one of the factors which led to the feud
between Freud and Jung was the latter's insistence on giving
psychological phenomena a degree of objectivity which Freud
found unacceptable.

Another, perhaps surprising, source of dissent is the discipline of
theoretical physics. There is a strong tradition of Platonism among
mathematicians. Those who fall into this camp tend to view new

developments in mathematics as discoveries rather than inventions. A similar tendency has been increasingly obvious in modern physics. Thus the mathematical physicist Roger Penrose asserts that 'whenever the mind perceives a mathematical idea it makes contact with Plato's world of mathematical concepts' (Penrose 1989, 428). Distinguished mathematicians such as Kurt Gödel (the discoverer/inventor of the incompleteness theorem) and René Thom (the author of the seminal work on catastrophe theory) also take a Platonic view of mathematics.[1] Similarly, John Polkinghorne asserts that

> we have good reason for supposing that there are inhabitants of the mental world which are not anchored in the material. The first candidates I would like to consider are the truths of mathematics. It is difficult to believe that they came into being with the action of the human mind that first thinks them. Rather their nature seems to be that of ever-existing realities which are discovered, but not constructed, by the explorations of the human mind.   (Polkinghorne 1988, 75)

He goes on to speak of the existence of a noetic realm 'in which we can participate without having created it or being able to exhaust its content, in much the same way that we participate in the physical world' (Polkinghorne 1988, 76)

A third source of dissenting voices is the so-called New Age movement. This remarkably diverse social and religious phenomenon defies any brief description. Suffice it to say that, with their speculations about elemental spirits and angels, about higher self and cosmic consciousness, New Agers represent a large and increasing body of Westerners who are no longer satisfied with materialism. Experimentation with drugs, meditation and other mind-altering techniques has led them on a quest for explanations which do not dismiss the spiritual as a mere epiphenomenon or by-product of matter. That quest for spiritualities which will help them to make sense of the increasingly post-modern world in which they live has led them to trawl the world's religious traditions.

Significantly, one tradition which New Agers have largely overlooked is that of Western Christianity.[2] This oversight is a judgement on a Church which has largely abandoned and/or privatized the more spiritual, supernatural aspects of Christianity. Many Western Christians are uncomfortable with the supernatural aspects of Christian faith and belief. Miracles, words of prophecy and personal spiritual entities (angels and demons) are reinterpreted figuratively or relegated safely to the past. Similarly, eschatology has for a long time been marginalized as an aspect of Christian teaching. These voices of dissent from the New Age, from theoretical physics and from psychoanalysis challenge our discomfort with the non-material dimensions of reality.

THE POWERS THAT BE

The inwardness of creation

The traditional view of heaven as 'a transcendent, otherworldly sphere qualitatively distinct from human life, to which the dead go if they have been good' (Wink 1984, 119) received short shrift during the modern era. Such a concept simply was not compatible with the closed and complete cosmos of classical physics. Thus it was an early casualty in the process of accommodating Christianity to modernity.

However, the metaphysical speculations of New Agers, the assertions of mathematicians and physicists that the laws of nature and the theorems are 'located' in a non-physical noetic realm, and Jung's popularization of a collective unconscious suggest that the time is ripe to reassess the concept of heaven and its marginalization over the last two centuries.

For traditional Christian theology, heaven was the invisible aspect of creation. Karl Barth describes it as 'the sum of all that which in creation is unfathomable, distant, alien and mysterious' (Barth 1960, 424).

More recently Walter Wink has proposed the metaphor of inwardness to 'locate' heaven. Thus heaven is to be understood as the 'within' of creation, its inscape. This metaphor has the advantage of reaffirming the traditional view of heaven as the invisible (i.e. non-physical) aspects of creation, while acting as a bridge to the views expressed by the dissenting voices mentioned above. Wink describes heaven thus: 'the metaphorical "place" in which the spirituality of everything is "located," as it were . . . the habitat of angels, spirits, cherubim, and seraphim, but also of demons and the devil and all the Powers "in the heavenly places" ' (Wink 1984, 119).

That latter description brings us to the denizens of heaven. For Jungians, archetypes would be among the inhabitants of the mystery of creation. Mathematical entities and laws of nature, the entities of Polkinghorne's noetic realm, would also be citizens of heaven. But how do they relate to the principalities, powers and angelic messengers who are, according to traditional theology, the inhabitants of these realms? The imagination of Christian artists over the centuries may have done us a disservice in portraying angels and demons as all too this-worldly realities. The literalistic modern mind has difficulty recognizing that the creatures with blackened leathery skin, vestigial bat-like wings and horned heads are to be taken as visual metaphors for spiritual realities. The Bible offers us no such portrayals. When its authors speak of angels they do not intend us to think of golden- and white-winged beings with pre-Raphaelite faces. 'Angel' simply means 'messenger' (as does the Hebrew counterpart *mal'ak*): they are spiritual realities functioning as God's messengers to us.

The spirituality of institutions

In his survey of New Testament terms for power, Walter Wink suggests that all human social and power structures have an interiority, a spiritual existence perhaps analogous to the human soul. Perhaps one might even extend this to natural and mathematical phenomena: might we not regard the laws of nature as the 'souls' of natural phenomena? This is not to suggest with Paul Dirac that a particular solution of Schrödinger's wave equation *is* the electron. However, it may be our best attempt to express the inwardness of an electron.

There are, of course, different ways of understanding this interiority. By implication, I have already ruled out the materialistic interpretation: that this is merely a by-product of physical reality. However, at least two other options come readily to mind.

One approach would be to ascribe such a degree of autonomy to the interiority that it comes to take priority over the physical phenomenon. The interiority becomes the ideal of which the phenomenon is merely the imperfect reflection. This kind of outlook led medieval theologians to suggest that God's idea of us is more real than our physical existence. Such an outlook easily gives rise to the sentiment that the body is the prison of the soul.

Wink, however, adopts another approach. He does not see either matter or spirit as having priority over the other. They are correlatives. Each one depends upon the other, and each one conditions the other. In a similar vein, Lesslie Newbigin speaks of principalities and powers as embodied in worldly realities:

> The principalities and powers are real. They are invisible and we cannot locate them in space. They do not exist as

disembodied entities floating above this world, or lurking within it. They meet us as embodied in visible and tangible realities – people, nations, and institutions. And they are powerful. (Newbigin 1989, 207)

Thus, in order to have an effect, they must be embodied. New Testament accounts of demon possession and exorcism suggest this very strongly. For example, the demons manifesting themselves through Legion plead with Jesus not be cast into a disembodied state – even embodiment in a herd of pigs is preferable to disembodiment (Mark 5.1–13). Similarly, racism as a disembodied idea is unpleasant, but this is a mere shadow of the demonic power of racism when embodied in social structures such as those of apartheid, Nazism or the British National Party.

Mentioning apartheid as a demonic power raises the question of what other spiritual powers can be identified in the modern world. If Wink is right, every social structure has a corresponding inwardness or spiritual power. Take, for example, multinational companies: every company has its own unique character, its own spirit which is stable and relatively autonomous of the employees at any particular time. Thus IBM, Ford and ICI each have their own distinctive characters. By extension, individual schools and hospitals and the educational and health systems in which they are embedded all have their own interiorities. Similarly, churches have their spirits or angels.[3]

One implication of this way of thinking is that such structures are relatively stable. The existence of an interior dimension lends the structure a high degree of protection against would-be reformers or revolutionaries who address themselves only to the externals. Having seized the reins of power, such people find the reins directing them! History is littered with accounts of well-intentioned people who thought they could change the system, only to be co-opted by it. For example, some years ago an acquaintance of mine was appointed to a difficult post; commenting on his success in the post some years later, a mutual friend observed that the job had moulded him into its shape. We often speak of mastering a particular job. More often the reality is that we adapt to it: the job masters us!

On a larger scale, each nation and culture will have its own interiority. Again, this is reflected in the biblical tradition of the angels of the nations. The angels or gods of the nations are not merely nationalistic myths but spiritual realities immanent within the social structures.

Their reality was made only too plain to Carl Jung in his experience of Nazi Germany. In 1936, at a time when many Christians still believed that Nazism was a viable answer to the creeping decadence and secularism of the modern world, Jung published a prophetic article simply entitled 'Wotan'. Rather than give a merely economic, political or psychological explanation for the phenomenon of Nazism, he postulated that a quasi-personal spiritual entity had taken possession of the German people. He identified it with Wotan, the chief god of the pre-Christian Teutons. Thus he could say 'a god has taken possession of the Germans and their house is filled with a "mighty rushing wind"' (Jung cited by Garrison 1982, 155–6). This was not mere metaphor; Jung repeatedly speaks of the Nazi phenomenon as *Ergriffenheit* (possession), with Wotan as the *Ergreifer* (the possessor) and Hitler in particular and the German people in general as the *Ergriffener* (the possessed).

The world system

Apartheid and Nazism together point to the demonic potential of the inner spiritual realities of our social structures. In his trilogy on the powers, Walter Wink explores at some length biblical teaching about the demon master, Satan. Drawing on that biblical background, he links together the individual fallen powers of human social structures in the following terms:

> I speak of 'demons' as the actual spirituality of systems and structures that have betrayed their divine vocations. I use the expression 'the Domination System' to indicate what happens when an entire network of Powers becomes integrated around idolatrous values. And I refer to 'Satan' as the world-encompassing spirit of the Domination System.   (Wink 1992, 8–9)

Elsewhere he identifies the domination system with what the New Testament and the early Church Fathers denote as 'the world' (*kosmos*). Thus the world is the entire network of human social and political structures in their rebellion against the intention of God. And the spirit of the world is named, both in the New Testament and in Wink's writings, as Satan.

Wink goes on to relate the overarching socio-cultural system called the world to the media. It is widely agreed that the media of mass communications are a major subsystem within the present global network of principalities and powers. Wink dwells on their role in propagating the myth which undergirds the domination system, namely, the myth of redemptive violence. The distinctive feature of this myth is that order is established in place of disorder by means of violence. It is the myth that legitimates the right of every American citizen to carry a gun. The myth of redemptive violence is the basis for the firm conviction that the appropriate response to a suspected act of Iraqi terrorism is the launching of 23 Cruise missiles against a residential suburb of Baghdad. But it is not just the news and party-political broadcasts which reinforce such a view. On the contrary, it is a central feature of much children's television. From Popeye and Batman to Teenage Mutant Hero Turtles and Thundercats the theme is the same: peace and order are threatened by evil beings who must be defeated by acts of violence. Such is the justification for the existence of organizations like the CIA: we must murder and destroy in order to preserve all that is true and good and beautiful. Commenting on contemporary American television, the senior Mennonite missiologist Wilbert Shenk has noted that 'Our children are being catechized, if you please, on violence'.[4]

Mammon

Another major subsystem within the present form of the domination system is the market. As I have already indicated, the global economic system is a central feature of modern life.

It possesses a high degree of autonomy relative to its participants. Not only individuals but even multinational corporations and governments appear relatively powerless in the face of market trends. Mrs Thatcher may have been expressing her free-market ideology, but there was more than an element of truth in her notorious 'You can't buck the market'. According to neo-classical economists the market is not governed by human planning, but by quasi-natural laws. For them the market is the realm of chance and necessity. Perhaps significantly Chance and Necessity were worshipped as divinities by our pre-modern ancestors. Lesslie Newbigin certainly perceives something of the same in modernity's attitude to the market: 'in our economic life we are no more responsible to Christ; we are not responsible at all, for economic life has been handed over to the goddess Fortuna' (Newbigin 1989, 207).

The sheer autonomy and complexity of the market make machine metaphors entirely inadequate. A more accurate picture would be that of an impersonal and amorphous but nevertheless powerful organic entity. Such an entity only too easily becomes the object of religious fervour (Seabrook 1990, 11).

The New Testament offers a very apt name for the underlying spirituality of the global economic system: Mammon. If Satan is the spiritual power behind or within the human world as a whole, Mammon is one of his chief angels.

The extent to which the market system and, hence, the spirit of Mammon has penetrated modern existence has already been indicated in some detail. Suffice it to recall that even those human institutions which have in the past stood apart from the market (e.g. our institutions of health and education) are increasingly dominated by market models. Thus considerations of human well-being are relativized by economic considerations. This man may benefit from a heart transplant, but is it cost-effective? Should Mr Smith, who earns twice as much, take a correspondingly higher place in the queue for a new kidney? Jane might find personal fulfilment in learning the play the cello, but what is the pay-off for society?

Similarly, our personal lives are dominated by the economic system. As we become increasingly dependent on money to pay for services which once we would have supplied for ourselves, we lose our autonomy. Fewer and fewer of us have the skill to repair a broken window or a faulty engine: we rely on our earnings to buy these services. Even the decision whether or not to have children is increasingly economic rather than a purely personal decision.

The competitiveness encouraged by the global economic system also has a destructive effect on relationships. At one time many people would have regarded their colleagues as friends. The impact of competition combined with the ultimacy of material success has left many people in business too busy watching their backs to develop any real friendships. Who can you trust? Your protégé may only too easily step into your shoes before you are ready to step out of them.

If Wink is right, it is not enough to look only at the political, economic and psychological factors involved in the market. The point of speaking about it as Mammon is to highlight that there is also a spiritual dimension which is not simply reducible to those other factors. Mammon is not merely a colourful metaphor for all that I have been describing. It is a spiritual reality undergirding those material realities. Any analysis which limits itself to the material aspects will be incomplete and to some extent inadequate.

The ambiguity of the powers

The easy option would be to set Christianity up as implacably opposed to the structures which order our fallen world. It is tempting to demonize the market, the media or the entire system. However, Christian theology does not permit us such an easy option.

On the contrary, the Bible (and following it Christian theology) consistently presents human beings as social creatures. We are not isolated individuals, but creatures who have been created to exist with each other and before God in a complex network of personal and social relationships. Our social structures and institutions are all expressions of that created sociality. Similarly, the undergirding principalities and powers, the spiritualities which inform our structures, are presented as capable of serving God's purposes. Both social structures and the corresponding spiritual realities[5] are part of God's good creation.

However, precisely because they are so closely related to our created humanity, our social structures and their interiorities partake in our human rebelliousness. They are fallen because we are fallen. Thus there is an ambiguity in every human institution (including the institution of the Church). Structures and their spirits may function as God intended them. Alternatively, they may become self-serving and, hence, demonic. Thus Wink defines 'demons' as 'the psychic or spiritual power emanated by organizations or individuals or subaspects of individuals whose energies are bent on overpowering others' (Wink 1984, 104), i.e. on mastering them and making them serve their own selfish ends.

It is this self-serving, this ambiguity, that is challenged by the ministry of Christ, not the existence of the powers as such. For example, we are told that 'having disarmed the powers and authorities, he made a public spectacle of them, triumphing over them by the cross' (Col 2.15). The image is of a Roman triumphal procession. Christ's victory has conquered the powers rather than annihilated them. The rebels have been subdued and made subject to Christ.

MISSION TO THE POWERS

The call of Christ

If Christ does not destroy the powers, but rather makes them submit to God's will, it follows that his call to us does not involve any call to implacable opposition to the structures of this world and their undergirding spirits. We are not called to usher in the kingdom by overthrowing the powers that be. Instead, we are called to demonstrate their subjection in Christ. We are called to live lives which show that the powers have no ultimate power over us or anyone else. It is a call to demonstrate the relativization of the powers.

But how are we to do this? Dietrich Bonhoeffer suggests that two essential components will be 'prayer and righteous action among men. All Christian thinking, speaking, and organizing, must be born anew out of this prayer and action' (Bonhoeffer 1971, 300).

Righteous action

In the course of the Sermon on the Mount, Jesus introduces two very important metaphors for righteous action. He calls upon his listeners to be the salt of the earth and the light of the world.

Salt was valued for its cleansing and purifying power. The call to be salt is a call to be purifying agents within society. It is a call to direct and indirect action influencing society for good and resisting evil. It requires much more of us than mere moral behaviour. It is a call to prophetic action.

Jesus gives various examples in the Sermon on the Mount: examples which have often been misinterpreted in a passive fashion. For example, the advice to go the second mile was not a suggestion that we should acquiesce in imperial injustice. On the contrary, it would have been an action which would have been very disturbing to the Roman soldier involved. The imperial authorities were becoming increasingly sensitive about the abuse of the power to press civilians into service. At the time of Christ there were already severe penalties for soldiers who were found to have exceeded their authority in this matter. Jesus is not saying 'Do him a favour', but rather 'Put him on the spot!' He is urging his listeners to a course of action which would certainly embarrass the soldier, and which might well put him at risk of disciplinary action.

Jesus also calls us to be light. He compares us with a city set on a hill: visible for miles around. We are to be beacons. But what are we to illuminate? I believe this is a call to us to model the kingdom of

God in the presence of this world. For example, in a culture which is increasingly fragmented and in which the community we all require for the full development of our humanity is increasingly hard to find, we are called to model true human community. This will not be an exclusive community, but one which welcomes the stranger.

Salt and light. Together they summarize the tension which is to characterize the Christian's life in the world. We are to be in the world but not of it. We are to be resident aliens. At one and the same time we are called to be salt (actively engaged in society, seeking to influence it for good) and light (set apart from our culture, modelling creative alternatives so that others may see in our works and our relationships the truth of the gospel).

Economics and righteous action

Turning to the specific example of our life within the economic structures of this culture, we are called to act against Mammon for Mammon. We are called to show in our lives and action that the market is not ultimate.

Prophetic leisure. One practical way of doing this is to engage in prophetic leisure. As Joseph Pieper argued in his classic *Leisure the Basis of Culture*, leisure is an essential feature of a fully human existence: 'the preserve of freedom, of education and culture, and of that undiminished humanity which views the world as a whole' (Pieper 1952, 59). However, we live in a hyperactive, workaholic culture which has reduced leisure to the status of preparation for work.

At a public level, we might demonstrate our commitment to leisure by resisting attempts to suppress a regular day of rest for the sake of purely economic interests. Keeping Sunday special is not a matter of imposing an archaic religious legalism upon a pagan culture. On the contrary, 'Sabbath rest is a revolutionary act. It defies the boundedness of the work-a-day world' (Edwards 1982, 8). Maintaining a day of rest is a public reminder that God, not the market, is ultimate – that Christ, not Mammon, is the Lord.

However, leisure is by no means mere absence of work. If we resist the ultimacy of work by maintaining a reasonable element of leisure in our lives, we will also want to make creative use of that time. One possibility is to devote some of our leisure to creating time and space for others. Thus hospitality is an important element of prophetic leisure. We demonstrate to others that we are not dominated by the world of work, by the market, when we show that we have time for them. Christian hospitality is an essential basis for community: personal relationships cannot develop without time, any more than flowers can grow without water.

Time for others may also be subversive: the experience of Eastern Europe is illuminating. It was as the churches gave the people of former Communist bloc countries such as East Germany time and space which was secure from the intrusion of the authorities that the protest movements began to flourish and the authoritarian structures began to crumble. Community may be about creating gaps in the institutional structures of modern life: gaps in which true humanity can flourish.

Christian simplicity.   Another form of prophetic action in the economic sphere is the practice of Christian simplicity. Simplicity of lifestyle has the potential to liberate us from bondage to commodities and success. Speaking from outside the Christian community, Jeremy Seabrook notes that

> The issue is not so much one of going 'beyond' the market economy, but rather of reducing it to a minimal, functional level in our lives, putting it in its (necessary) place. At present, it is allowed free passage into deeper and deeper places in the heart, imagination and spirit of people. By resisting this process, we might well discover areas of autonomy, independence and inventiveness that have been put to sleep through our automatic surrender to the invasion of a dispossessing enrichment, a pauperizing wealth, which we have come to accept as part of a 'natural' process. The greatest lesson might be, not how little we can achieve without a lot of money, but how much we can accomplish with relatively little.   (Seabrook 1990, 33)

The practice of simplicity is such a relativizing of the market. By freeing us from the need to compete, it sets us free to befriend our colleagues, to begin to rebuild community in our places of work. By freeing us from the glamour of commodities, it makes it easier for us to open our eyes to the economic injustices which are practised on the behalf of the West. If we are free from the shackles of getting and spending, we are also free to follow our consciences. Thus it puts Christians in a stronger position to blow the whistle on injustices and illegalities perpetrated by their employers.

Simplicity and leisure on their own are examples of being salt in the world. However, they may also be part of a package of actions intended to model an alternative economic system. There is tremendous scope for the development of a Christian economics.[6] Such a system might well pick up biblical concepts such as stewardship, *shalom*, (peace, wholeness, health, social justice) and community.

Prayer

An analysis of social and cultural structures which includes the spiritual dimension will inevitably highlight the need for prayer. Action to change structures is necessary but not sufficient. Jung's comments on the re-emergence of Wotan within the German psyche are significant:

> He simply disappeared when times turned against him, and remained invisible for more than a thousand years, working anonymously and indirectly. Archetypes are like riverbeds which dry up when the water deserts them, but which it can find at any time. An archetype is like an old watercourse along which the water of life has flowed for centuries, digging a deep channel for itself. The longer it has flowed in this channel the more likely it is that sooner or later the water will return to its old bed. (Jung cited by Garrison 1982, 155)

With the arrival of Christianity, the water was diverted. But Wotan was not destroyed. The spiritual potential for Nazism remained submerged within German hearts. Some years later Jung commented that Christianity had suppressed the ancient brutality of the Teutons. He regarded the subsequent demise of Christianity as the precursor for the re-emergence of that brutality.

Analysis of society and culture in terms of spiritual powers reminds us that in addition to structural change there also has to be a change of heart. This is true at the individual level: changes in outward behaviour are of little significance if there has been no change of heart. If we think of the principalities and powers as immanent in social structures, a similar transformation of the inner reality is called for.

However, it is beyond our powers to effect such an inner transformation. Thus we are forced to prayer; to dialogue with the one who alone has the power to effect such changes.

Walter Wink describes intercession as spiritual defiance. It is certainly an act which stems from a deep dissatisfaction with the status quo and a realistic assessment of one's own very limited capacity to effect change.

The fact that today many Christians are uncomfortable with the idea of intercessory prayer (and still more with exorcism and spiritual warfare) is one more example of the inroads which modernity has made into the churches. Modernity effectively outlawed prayer. One of the most pressing tasks of the Church in the last days of the modern era is to rediscover the discipline and power of prayer.

NOTES

1. In Gödel's case, he justifies his Platonism by reference to the incompleteness of mathematical systems. In any mathematical system, there will always be statements which are true but not provable from axioms derived from that system. Thus he envisaged such unprovable truths as already existing in a Platonic sphere.
2. Eastern Orthodoxy and the more mystical forms of Roman Catholicism have attracted rather more attention (probably because of the romance surrounding them rather than any inherent affinity to New Age ideas).
3. Belief in angels as guardians and guarantors of the proper order of worship is apparent in the New Testament (e.g. 1 Cor 11.10; Rev 2 – 3) and was to become commonplace among the Church Fathers.
4. Shenk makes this remark in the course of the video *It's No Good Shouting*.
5. In biblical terms, the angels of the nations, the angels of the churches, etc.
6. It is one of the peculiarities of modernity that 'Christian' economics is likely to ridiculed as a contradiction in terms (an illegitimate mixing of the public and private spheres) whereas no contradiction is perceived in having a chair in Islamic economics at a British university.

CHAPTER 16

From Interdependence
to Relationship

EXPLORATIONS OF INTERDEPENDENCE

It is sometimes said that 'there are only three possible ways of understanding the world: the atomic, the oceanic, and the relational – symbolized respectively by billiard balls, the ocean and the net' (Newbigin 1989, 171–2).

The billiard-ball model of the world is only too familiar. It is the world of modernity which has dominated so much of this book. It has proved a tremendously powerful tool for mastering the physical world. But our culture has succumbed to the very human temptation to take a good thing to excess. In the world of late modernity many are turning away in dissatisfaction from atomistic visions of reality.

Contemporary culture is rife with explorations of alternative ways of understanding the world. These range from the highly disciplined approach of systems thinking, which has proved invaluable in opening up our understanding of complex physical, biological and social systems, to the entirely undisciplined explorations of mysticism and esoteric spirituality which characterize the New Age.

In view of such a shift in our culture's understanding of the world, it is worthwhile recalling that Christianity emerged in a variety of cultural contexts which were, generally speaking, more relational in their outlook. Thus we may find in the Christian traditions various resources for a more holistic understanding of the world.

INTERDEPENDENCE IN CHRISTIAN THOUGHT

Peace in the Old Testament

The Hebrew concept of *shalom* or peace contrasts sharply with the classical Greek concept of *eirēnē* (also translated 'peace'). The latter has primarily negative connotations: peace is understood as the absence of war or violence.

Shalom, however, is a positive concept which might well have been translated as 'wholeness' or 'harmony'. It is also a very wide-ranging concept. The Old Testament notion of peace is a state of well-being which embraces physical health, psychological and spiritual well-being, material prosperity, social justice and harmony, and harmony with the environment in addition to the usual understanding of peace between warring factions or nations.

The Church as a body

Among Hellenistic Jews the Septuagint translation of *shalom* as *eirēnē* allowed the latter concept to be filled out with the positive content of the former. As a result, when peace appears in the New Testament it is better understood in terms of its Jewish cultural context than in terms of its classical Greek etymology.

Another important biblical resource for the development of a more relational approach to reality is the New Testament's use of body as a metaphor for church. Those who are called out by God (*ek-klēsia*) to become the Christian community, the anticipation here and now of the kingdom of God, are presented as existing in relationships of mutual dependence.

This implies a differentiation of function in which every member has his or her own unique place: 'If they were all one part, where would the body be? As it is, there are many parts, but one body' (1 Cor 12.19–20). Contrast this with the relative uniformity of many of our churches. The suppression of diversity is characteristic of a system organized on atomistic lines to establish and maintain domination over others. A community of mutual dependence cannot coexist with a hierarchically ordered system of power over others.

Clearly, if we were to take the biblical metaphor at all seriously, it would have far-reaching implications for our understanding of the Church.

One God in three persons

However, even the metaphor of a harmoniously functioning body is not the most fundamental Christian resource for a relational understanding of the world. That distinction goes to the orthodox Christian doctrine of God as Trinity.

The doctrine of the Trinity has until relatively recently been a Cinderella doctrine, at least in Western Christianity. It is generally regarded as too abstract and difficult to be taught to 'mere lay people', and even clergy will admit without embarrassment to a lack of understanding at this point. And yet this doctrine was held, by those who developed it, to be absolutely fundamental to Christian faith *and practice*. It was regarded as the defining characteristic of authentic Christianity.

If forced to expound the doctrine, most Western Christians would probably respond by suggesting that there is one God who somehow manifests himself in three ways as Father, Son and Holy Spirit (or, in less sexist but also more abstract terms, as Creator, Redeemer and Life-giver). Not only is this a classical heresy, but it is almost the reverse of what the orthodox doctrine of the Trinity actually says.

According to orthodox trinitarianism there are three divine persons who are so related that we must speak of them as one God. Unity is a function of the interrelatedness of three irreducible particulars. What this does is to make personal relationship fundamental to the nature of God and, hence, to the nature of created reality.

The image of God

One of the fundamental biblical ways of talking about human nature is as 'the image of God'. This has been interpreted in many different ways by Christian theologians. However, in the light of what has just been said about personal relatedness being fundamental to the nature of God, the most convincing interpretation is that which takes its cue from the parallelism between 'image of God' and 'male and female' in Genesis 1.27. Whatever else it might mean, this surely indicates that being the image of God entails personal relationship.

188   *Restoring the vision*

THE HEALING OF RELATIONSHIPS

Good news

Jesus came preaching good news. Subsequently his life and ministry have become the basis for the good news which we are called to share.

With the advent of liberation theology it has become fashionable to characterize the good news as news of liberation. The message we are commissioned to proclaim is a promise of liberation. Precisely what we feel we need to be liberated from is a matter that has varied from culture to culture.

Throughout the ages some people have perceived that ignorance is what imprisons them. Such people have tended to see the gospel as *gnōsis*; special privileged knowledge which enables the imprisoned soul to break free from the material world. In some of its forms this has produced a spiritual élitism which Christian orthodoxy has rightly questioned.

Others have seen threatening cosmic forces as the source of our bondage. For them, Christ's death and resurrection represent a decisive victory over the principalities and powers.

A more common point of view today would be to see the brokenness of our world as the source of our bondage.

Common to these ways of perceiving that from which we need to be liberated is the experience of oppressive relationships. We exist within a network of exploitative relationships and we too participate in the exploitation of others within the network. The gospel promises liberation from such a system.

However, this is merely the negative aspect of liberation. To be meaningful there must be a positive content as well. The good news we have to share would not be good news if it only promised the dissolution of oppressive relationships. This would instead be the dubious promise of release from oppressive but familiar and therefore comfortable relationships into an uncertain wilderness of undefined relationships. Oppressive order is for most people preferable to chaos, be it ever so liberating.

However, the gospel does have a positive content. It is good news of Jesus Christ, or good news of the kingdom. This is not some vague and undefined future state. On the contrary, the kingdom is anticipated in the Church: the *body* of men and women who have been called by God into a new network of relationships. More explicitly, it is the 'gospel of peace' (Eph 6.15).

Thus the gospel's promise of liberation is not from oppressive relationships into an uncertain future. It is the promise of the restoration of *shalom*. The gospel is good news of wholeness and harmony. It promises a restored relationship with God; no matter how individualistic or atomistic Christianity has become, at least that dimension has been a recurring feature. But *shalom* also holds out a promise of physical and psychological wholeness: of reconciliation with our self. Nor does it stop there. In its fullness, the restoration of *shalom* includes reconciliation with our fellow creatures. This will involve the establishment of social harmony and justice through non-oppressive relationships. It will even extend to a harmonious relationship with the natural environment – understood not as a human resource, but as God's good creation, and therefore with an integrity of its own which relativizes any 'rights' we may presume to have over it.

The Christian healing ministry

Following Jesus' example, there is a long and honourable tradition of healing within the Christian churches. Today it is often seen as part of the churches' pastoral ministry. However, this manifestation of reconciliation should not be confined to those already within the Christian community.

It is an integral part of the priesthood of all believers to engage in healing and reconciliation at all levels. It is part of what it means for the Christian community to be open to the world.

Our calling is not just to proclaim the establishment of renewed relationships, but to act for their establishment. As I have already indicated, such action must take place at the secular and spiritual levels simultaneously: prayer *and* righteous action.

As Christian communities, we begin to realize the kingdom of God when we pray and act to restore relationships of all kinds.

SPIRITUALITY: PERSONAL, *NOT* INDIVIDUAL

Spirituality is fashionable today. Millions of people are turning away in disgust from the materialism of late modernity. Indeed its popularity is such as to raise serious questions about theories of secularization.

Ironically, one of the driving forces behind this renewal of interest in the world of the spirit has been the imperialism of modern science. Not content with applying the scientific method to the physical world, scientists have progressively applied it in the study of humans themselves, both individually and corporately. Thus Sigmund Freud and Carl Jung clearly undertook their pioneering explorations of the psyche in a scientific spirit. This is seen, for example, in the empiricism which characterizes much modern psychoanalysis.

Another assumption of the scientific world-view which has found its way into psychoanalysis and thence into the contemporary resurgence of spirituality is its individualism.[1] The new spiritualities, like psychoanalysis and the human potential movement, are primarily concerned with the quest for *self*-fulfilment, with the process of individuation.

The paradox of Christian spirituality

'If anyone would come after me, he must deny himself and take up his cross and follow me. For whoever wants to save his life will lose it, but whoever loses his life for me and for the gospel will save it.'   (Mark 8.34b–35)

According to Jesus, the kind of concentration upon self encouraged by so many of the new spiritualities is ultimately futile. On the contrary, in order to find ourselves we must first be prepared to lose ourselves.

Many critics have dismissed this as nothing more than self-hatred. Sadly, this criticism would appear to be amply justified by the excesses of asceticism which are to be found within the history of Christianity.

However, self-denial is no more than a preliminary stage. If self-fulfilment is futile as an end in itself, so is self-denial. The latter is merely the mirror image of the former. Hence Jesus' reference to the cross. He highlights the fact that genuine personal growth is not to be achieved by our own efforts, either positive or negative. The way of the cross is a radical discontinuity. It is for all who have come to a dead end in their personal development. At that point the only way forward is this most radical of steps: the abandonment of the quest! It means allowing all our hopes to be put to death with Christ.

But the way of the cross extends beyond death. In embracing Christ's cross we are also embracing his resurrection. Beyond death there is the promise of a life in which we are enabled to fulfil that vocation: 'Follow me.'

In our individualistic culture, those words inevitably take on individualistic overtones. But we must remember that the context in which they were spoken by Jesus was very different from our own.

The call to follow Christ is not a call to some private spiritual pilgrimage. On the contrary, pilgrimage is a social concept. The

Bible knows nothing of solitary pilgrimages. In the biblical records, when journeys with a spiritual dimension are undertaken, they are almost invariably undertaken by an entire community. For example, Abraham left his ancestral home in response to the call of God. But he did not go alone. His entire household, an extended family of some considerable size, went with him.

This reflects one of the most fundamental biblical assumptions about what it is to be human. As human beings we are called to image a personal God. Over the centuries Christians have offered many alternative explanations of what it means to image God. But the one that most closely reflects what the biblical texts actually say about the image of God is that we image God by being in personal relationship with one another: 'God created man in his own image, in the image of God he created him; male and female he created them' (Gen 1.27).

Following Christ cannot be divorced from this fundamental human vocation to be persons-in-relationship. The American pastoral theologian Herb Anderson suggests that we must learn to live together separately (Anderson 1984, 15). He is referring to family life, but it applies equally well to all social dimensions of human life.

Relational spirituality

It follows from the fundamental nature of being-in-relationship that Christian spirituality is inescapably social or relational. This should be true at all times and in all places, but it is particularly important in a culture which is undergoing a dramatic fragmentation of human community combined with an upsurge of interest in spirituality.

It means that Christian spirituality is not merely a matter of promoting private prayer and other spiritual practices. It must also find expression in our living together in transformed relationships. It means the abandonment of relationships of domination in favour of relationships of mutuality.

Thus Christian spirituality is not just about prayer, it is also about living together in our families and personal friendships. It is not just about 'the inner life', it is about living with others before God in every sphere of life. Christian spirituality is not about individualistic enlightenment, but about the discovery of God even in the trivia of the daily routine and the inconvenience of living with others.

The importance of the social dimension in Christian spirituality is underlined by the long tradition of religious life. Indeed, religious life has become virtually synonymous with life in community. Even the desert fathers, with their emphasis on solitude, developed a loose community existence. Solitude is regarded as exceptional in most religious orders, and a vocation to solitude will be tested very rigorously before it is ratified by the community.[2]

It follows that Christian spirituality cannot be divorced from membership of the Church, the community of those who have been called by God. As Lesslie Newbigin points out, 'the developing, nourishing, and sustaining of Christian faith and practice is impossible apart from the life of a believing congregation' (Newbigin 1989, 235). This is the truth hidden in the old Roman Catholic dictum that 'There is no salvation outside the Church'. The imperialistic overtones of this assertion all too easily blind us to the fact that for an essentially social faith there can be no wholeness outside the community.

Finally, Christian spirituality cannot be divorced from life in the wider community. In our accommodation to modernity we have found it only too easy to limit it to the private sphere of the family and leisure. But the biblical authors never limited it in this way. Those who are blessed by the Father are those to whom the Son of Man says 'I was hungry and you gave me something to eat, I was thirsty and you gave me something to drink, I was a stranger and you invited me in, I needed clothes and you clothed me, I was sick and you looked after me, I was in prison and you came to visit me' (Matt 25.35–36). Thus authentic Christian spirituality is inescapably political spirituality.

COMMUNITY AS THE MEDIUM OF THE GOSPEL

Rediscovering community

Unfortunately, the community dimension of Christian spirituality is missing from many of our churches. A weekly meeting for worship, safely isolated from each other by Victorian pews, is not community.

The call to proclaim the gospel in our culture must include a call to rediscover Christian community in our culture.

One fundamental feature of human community is eating together. Both Jesus and his detractors defined him by who he ate with: outcasts and sinners. A good way of identifying the communities to which you belong is to ask with whom you eat. In an age of nearly instant TV dinners the answer is only too often that we no longer eat together: we may eat in the same room and at the same time, but because of the television we are no longer together.

Taking time to eat with family and friends is essential to the development of relationships at that personal level. But eating together is also vital to the development of community within religious orders and local congregations. At one time celebrating the eucharist together fulfilled that function, but for many of us it has been so individualized that it is now impossible for us to think of it as a community event. There is a simple point to all this: if we want to rediscover community in our congregations, we must seek appropriate ways of being together. Simple fellowship meals and times of communal celebration are important parts of such a process.

But being community is not all that is involved in being the community God has called us to be. I know of entirely secular organizations (e.g. certain choirs and political associations) which have a stronger communal existence than most of the churches I have experienced. The difference lies in our openness to others. The Church is not a religious club which defines its membership in the usual exclusive way, by identifying the characteristics of those who do or do not belong. On the contrary, the Church is a community which exists for the sake of those who are not its members. Thus Lesslie Newbigin makes the very important point that:

> If the gospel is to challenge the public life of our society . . . it will not be by forming a Christian political party, or by aggressive propaganda campaigns . . .
>
> It will only be by movements that begin with the local congregation in which the reality of the new creation is present, known, and experienced, and from which men and women will go into every sector of public life to claim it for Christ, to unmask the illusions which have remained hidden and to expose all areas of public life to the illumination of the gospel. But that will only happen as and when congregations renounce an introverted concern for their own life, and recognize that they exist for the sake of those who are not members, as sign, instrument, and foretaste of God's redeeming grace for the whole life of society. (Newbigin 1989, 233)

Finally, it should be noted that the Church of God, the community of those who have been called, cannot simply be identified with the institutional structures of our churches. An archdeacon recently commented to my wife that very often the most exciting developments in Christianity occur outside the denominational structures. That comment is amply justified by church history. At the risk of generalizing, I would venture to say that none of the great movements for renewal and revival which have nourished the Church throughout its history has been the child of the institutional Church. This is not to deny the value of institutions: they provide the form. If you like, they are the bones on which the body of Christ grows and without which it would get nowhere. But in a healthy body the bones should be invisible. And bones on their own constitute nothing more than a long-dead corpse. The institutions are nothing without the life-giving activity of the Holy Spirit breathing through them.

Hospitality as evangelism

Churches are called to be Christian communities. In our culture this means that we are called to model human community for the many whose experience of community has been limited or negative. Thus our communities must be open to the stranger and alien.

Hospitality is a traditional Christian ministry. Basically this is the creation of a welcoming space for people (Nouwen 1976, 64, 68).

Various things can threaten the friendliness of the space we create, can undermine our efforts to be hospitable.

Hospitality is threatened when the space we create is over-structured: we make people welcome but insist that they adapt to an already existing way of doing things. This is true of many traditional institutional churches. Very few Christians would admit that they actively discourage outsiders from participating in their communities. However, we expect outsiders to conform to our well-established religious sub-culture. Unfortunately our religious sub-cultures are often so out of touch with the surrounding secular culture that visitors to our churches (or even to Christian homes) experience something akin to culture shock.

Alternatively, hospitality is threatened by too much intimacy. This may seem surprising, conditioned as we are to think of hospitality exclusively in terms of welcoming someone into the privacy of our home with a view to establishing and developing friendship. However, as Patrick Keifert points out, there is more to hospitality than welcoming people into our private space:

> the response of hospitality to the stranger can by no means be limited to the specific one-to-one friendly encounters we

usually imagine by this metaphor. Hospitality to the stranger is critical to public life by definition, because it is precisely the interaction of strangers through a common set of actions that constitutes a public. Where there is no space for strangers, there can be no public. (Keifert 1992, 8)

In other words, hospitality is also about the creation or re-creation of public spaces in a culture which has seen the steady erosion of public space. We do no service to people who are already trapped in a network of private spaces by merely offering them the opportunity to belong to yet another exclusive club.

Finally, hospitality may be threatened by under-structuring. As Os Guinness has pointed out, one of the factors which puts the contemporary family under so much stress is the lack of structure in our private spaces. Henri Nouwen comments that a space without structure is not a welcoming home but a haunted house. Merely providing strangers with a space in which they can do their own thing without encountering us is not Christian hospitality.[3]

Thus Christian hospitality requires a certain minimum structure. To begin with, it requires that we give the stranger room to tell their own story. We must listen and welcome and seek to understand the stranger's story. We must listen, for it may be that God wishes to speak to us through the stranger. Karl Barth, a theologian not usually associated with the belief that God can speak through means other than Scripture, was, in fact, quite clear on this point:

In the very light of this narrower and smaller sphere of the Bible and the Church, we cannot possibly think that He cannot speak, and His speech cannot be attested, outside this sphere. We who in contrast to others have our place and our task here, and to whom it is given to know what others do not know, can and must expect that His voice will also be heard without. (Barth 1961, 117)

Or, as the Bible itself has it: 'Do not forget to entertain strangers, for by so doing some people have entertained angels without knowing it' (Heb 13.2).

Hospitality requires that we listen respectfully to the other's story. But it also requires that we allow room for our own story. In other words, the practice of Christian hospitality entails the articulation of the gospel as it has impacted upon our own lives. As Henri Nouwen comments, 'it belongs to the core of Christian spirituality to reach out to the other with good news and to speak without embarrassment about what we "have heard and . . . seen with our own eyes . . . watched and touched with our hands" (1 John 1:1)' (Nouwen 1976, 92).

Genuine hospitality is not about the avoidance of confrontation. Personal relationships do not develop if we carry on in a state of anxiety, always trying to skirt gingerly around potential areas of disagreement. In a marriage, personal growth depends upon acknowledging our disagreements and being prepared to work through those disagreements, sometimes to agreement but sometimes agreeing to differ. Similarly, genuine hospitality creates the possibility for such legitimate confrontation: the confrontation in love that is a prerequisite for genuine dialogue.

In the course of such dialogue we are sowing the seed of the gospel. In allowing our guests to encounter us as persons who have been and are being transformed by Christ, we create opportunities for them to encounter Christ for themselves. But our vocation is only to sow seed. We have no right to dictate how that seed might be received. We are not called to judge the response of others. We are sowers, not weeders.

NOTES

1. For example, Theodore Roszak has recently criticized psychoanalysis for its lack of social and ecological dimensions (Roszak 1992).
2. For example, Thomas Merton's struggles with his Trappist community.
3. *Pace* St James's, Piccadilly and its policy of providing space for all kinds of alternatives to traditional Christian belief.

Gospel & Culture

Christian Mission in the
Western World

A decade of development

In the early 1980s, concern for Christian witness in Western culture reached new levels of intensity. The churches appeared to lack a clear Christian perspective on issues affecting the future of modern culture. This seemed to correlate with the growing invisibility of the Church in Western culture and the steady drift of people away from active participation in church life.

In seeking to address these concerns, the British Council of Churches (now the Council of Churches for Britain and Ireland) commissioned Bishop Lesslie Newbigin to draft a programme statement defining the issues that needed to be addressed. This statement was subsequently published as *The Other Side of 1984: Questions for the Churches* (Geneva: WCC, 1983).

The response to that booklet was so strong that the BCC authorized the formation of The Gospel and Our Culture programme. It was established with a national consultation in July 1992 as the climax. As the programme evolved, the theme for this consultation emerged as 'The Gospel as Public Truth'.

Bishop Newbigin took an active part both in the development of the programme and in the broader ground-swell of concern about the relationship between contemporary culture and the Christian gospel. With the first co-ordinator of the programme, Dan Beeby, he worked tirelessly to bring these issues to as wide an audience as possible, both in the UK and abroad. One fruit of his efforts has been the publication of several books addressing these issues: *Foolishness to the Greeks* (1986), *The Gospel in a Pluralist Society* (1989) and *Truth to Tell* (1991).

Besides the national consultation, The Gospel and Our Culture has organized three regional conferences in co-operation with the British and Foreign Bible Society and the National Bible Society of Scotland.

The 1992 Consultation brought together academic, church and public leaders to examine the issues at the heart of contemporary culture in light of the Christian gospel, especially as these bear on the welfare of the whole of society. In preparation, eight study groups explored the issues to be addressed at the consultation: epistemology, history, science, the arts, economics, education, health and healing, and the media. Members of these groups were invited to write position papers which were subsequently edited by Bishop Hugh Montefiore and published under the title *The Gospel and Contemporary Culture* (Mowbray, 1992) as the study volume for the consultation.

Others have become involved, both nationally and internationally. For example, an international group of missiologists has responded to this initiative by setting up a long-term project to develop 'A Missiology for Western Culture'. Closer to home, it has led to a widely used parish study course (John de Wit, *Another Way of Looking* (BFBS, 1990)), while another clergyman has been exploring the implications for evangelism within the parish.

Because the issues addressed are of international concern, parallel movements have sprung up in several other countries. For example, there is now a very active Gospel and Our Culture Network in North America and a Gospel and Cultures Trust in New Zealand. Elsewhere, interest in the issues raised by The Gospel and Our Culture has been expressed from as far afield as Finland and South Africa, Taiwan and Croatia.

The way ahead

The programme was originally intended to cease at the end of the 1992 Consultation. However, because of the response to the consultation, it will now continue as a resource group at the service of the churches for their mission to contemporary culture. To that end, it has been reconstituted as a charitable company.

The primary aim of the programme is to encourage a critical re-examination and reform of the fundamental presuppositions of our culture. To fulfil this aim, The Gospel and Our Culture has set itself several tasks:

(1) the identification of allies in the different dimensions of our culture and within the churches;
(2) the encouragement of existing initiatives which overlap with our own aim;
(3) the development of a network of those committed to the aims and objectives of the programme in various ways: those actively engaged in their own place in the interests of the programme; those who might link the programme with other work, or provide entry into new areas; and those interested in a more general way;
(4) the publication of a quarterly newsletter, focusing on different aspects of the relationship between the gospel and our culture, and keeping subscribers informed of events, conferences, new books, opportunities for further study, exploration or action;
(5) further conferences and consultations.

The Gospel and Our Culture has recently merged with the C.S. Lewis Centre under the new name Gospel & Culture in order to pursue these aims more effectively. For more information about the work of the new organization, please contact the Director of Gospel & Culture.

Dr Andrew Walker
CES
King's College London
Waterloo Road
London
SE1 8TX

References

J.A. Aagard (1982) 'Hinduism's world mission', *Update*, 6 no. 3, 4–9.

H. Anderson (1984) *The Family and Pastoral Care* (Philadelphia: Fortress Press).

B. Appleyard (1992) *Understanding the Present: Science and Soul of Modern Man* (London: Picador).

J. Baillie (1950) *The Belief in Progress* (London: Oxford University Press).

R. Banks (1983) *The Tyranny of Time* (Exeter: Paternoster).

I.G. Barbour (1966) *Issues in Science and Religion* (London: SCM).

J.D. Barrow and F.J. Tipler (1986) *The Anthropic Cosmological Principle* (Oxford: Clarendon Press).

K. Barth (1960) *Church Dogmatics*, Vol. 3: *The Doctrine of Creation*, Part 3, tr. G.W. Bromiley and R.J. Ehrlich (Edinburgh: T. & T. Clark).

—— (1961) *Church Dogmatics*, Vol. 4: *The Doctrine of Reconciliation*, Part 3 (1st half), tr. G.W. Bromiley and R.J. Ehrlich (Edinburgh: T. & T. Clark).

D. Bebbington (1979) *Patterns in History* (Leicester: Inter-Varsity Press).

J. Begbie (1992) 'The Gospel, the arts and our culture' in Montefiore (1992), 58–83.

V. Blackmore and A. Page (1989) *Evolution: The Great Debate* (Oxford: Lion).

D. Bonhoeffer (1971) *Letters and Papers from Prison* (enlarged edition), ed. E. Bethge (London: SCM).

D.J. Bosch (1979) *A Spirituality of the Road* (Scottdale, PA: Herald Press).

—— (1991) *Transforming Mission: Paradigm Shifts in the Theology of Mission* (Maryknoll, NY: Orbis).

J.B. Bury (1920) *The Idea of Progress: An Inquiry into Its Origin and Growth* (London: Macmillan & Co.).

F. Capra (1982) *The Turning Point: Science, Society and the Rising Culture* (London: Wildwood House).

J. Collier (1992) 'Contemporary culture and the role of economics' in Montefiore (1992), 103–28.

R.G. Collingwood (1945) *The Idea of Nature* (Oxford).

R. Descartes (1968) *Discourse on Method and the Meditations*, tr. F.E. Sutcliffe (Harmondsworth: Penguin).

T. Eagleton and B. Wicker (eds) (1968) *From Culture to Revolution: The Slant Symposium 1967* (London: Sheed & Ward).

T. Edwards (1982) 'The Christian Sabbath: its promise today as a basic spiritual discipline', *Worship*, 56, 2–18.

M. Fox (1988) *The Coming of the Cosmic Christ: The Healing of Mother Earth and the Birth of a Global Renaissance* (San Francisco: Harper & Row).

D.A. Fraser and D.A. Campolo (1992) *Sociology Through the Eyes of Faith* (Leicester: Apollos).

F. Fukuyama (1989) 'The end of history?', *The National Interest* (Summer 1989), 3–18.

J. Garrison (1982) *The Darkness of God: Theology After Hiroshima* (London: SCM).

L. Gilkey (1976) *Reaping the Whirlwind: A Christian Interpretation of History* (New York: Seabury Press).

GPT (1992) Transcript of plenary addresses from 'The Gospel as Public Truth: Swanwick 1992' (Swindon: British and Foreign Bible Society).

O. Guinness (1983) *The Gravedigger File* (London: Hodder).

C.E. Gunton (1985) *Enlightenment and Alienation: An Essay Towards a Trinitarian Theology* (Basingstoke: Marshall Pickering).

—— (1992) 'Knowledge and culture: towards an epistemology of the concrete' in Montefiore (1992), 84–102.

C.E. Gunton and D.W. Hardy (eds) (1989) *On Being the Church: Essays on the Christian Community* (Edinburgh: T. & T. Clark).

D. Harvey (1990) *The Condition of Postmodernity* (Oxford: Blackwell).

I. Illich (1971) *Deschooling Society* (Harmondsworth: Penguin, 1973).
E. Ives (1992) 'The Gospel and history' in Montefiore (1992), 13–39.

R.W. Jenson (1973) *Story and Promise: A Brief Theology of the Gospel About Jesus* (Philadelphia: Fortress).
—— (1992) *Unbaptized God: The Basic Flaw in Ecumenical Theology* (Minneapolis: Augsburg Fortress).
G. Josipovici (1988) *The Book of God: A Response to the Bible* (New Haven: Yale University Press).

C.B. Kaiser (1991) *Creation and the History of Science* (*History of Christian Theology*, ed P. Avis, Vol. 3; London: Marshall Pickering).
I. Kant (1933) *Critique of Pure Reason*, tr. Norman Kemp Smith (London: Macmillan).
—— (1970) 'An answer to the question "What is enlightenment" ' in *Kant's Political Writings*, ed. H. Reiss (Cambridge: Cambridge University Press).
P.R. Keifert (1992) *Welcoming the Stranger: A Public Theology of Worship and Evangelism* (Minneapolis: Fortress).
A. Koyré (1957) *From the Closed World to the Infinite Universe* (Baltimore: The John Hopkins Press).
T.S. Kuhn (1970) *The Structure of Scientific Revolutions* (2nd edition; Chicago: University of Chicago Press).

K. Leech (1993) *The Eye of the Storm: Spiritual Resources for the Pursuit of Justice* (London: Darton, Longman & Todd).
A.O. Lovejoy (1936) *The Great Chain of Being: A Study of the History of an Idea* (Cambridge, MA: Harvard University Press).

R. May (1975) *The Courage to Create* (New York: W.W. Norton).
J. Monod (1974) *Chance and Necessity: An Essay on the Natural Philosophy of Modern Biology* (London: Fontana).
H. Montefiore (ed.) (1992) *The Gospel and Contemporary Culture* (London: Mowbray).

L. Newbigin (1983) *The Other Side of 1984: Questions for the Churches* (Geneva: WCC).
—— (1989) *The Gospel in a Pluralist Society* (London: SPCK).
—— (1990) 'Muslims, Christians and public doctrine', *The Gospel and Our Culture Newsletter*, no. 6, 1–2.
—— (1991a) *Truth to Tell: The Gospel as Public Truth* (London: SPCK).
—— (1991b) 'Response to criticisms of "The Gospel as Public Truth" ', *The Gospel and Our Culture Newsletter*, no. 10, 2–3.
H.R. Niebuhr (1951) *Christ and Culture* (New York: Harper & Row).
—— (1959) *The Kingdom of God in America* (New York: Harper & Row).

F. Nietzsche (1977) *The Nietzsche Reader*, sel. R.J. Hollingdale (Harmondsworth: Penguin).
H. Nouwen (1976) *Reaching Out: The Three Movements of the Spiritual Life* (London: Collins).

O. O'Donovan (1986) *Resurrection and Moral Order: An Outline of Evangelical Ethics* (Leicester: Inter-Varsity Press).
L.H. Osborn (1993) *Guardians of Creation: Nature in Theology and the Christian Life* (Leicester: Apollos).

J. Pelikan (1971) *The Christian Tradition*, 1: *The Emergence of the Catholic Tradition (100–600)* (Chicago: University of Chicago Press).
—— (1984) *The Christian Tradition*, 4: *Reformation of Church and Dogma (1300–1700)* (Chicago: University of Chicago Press).
R. Penrose (1989) *The Emperor's New Mind: Concerning Computers, Minds and the Laws of Physics* (Oxford: Oxford University Press).
J. Pieper (1952) *Leisure the Basis of Culture* (London: Faber & Faber).
M. Polanyi (1958) *Personal Knowledge: Towards a Post-Critical Philosophy* (London: Routledge & Kegan Paul).
J. Polkinghorne (1988) *Science and Creation: The Search for Understanding* (London: SPCK).
A. Pope (1733) 'Essay on Man' in *The Oxford Authors: Alexander Pope*, ed. P. Rogers (Oxford: Oxford University Press), 271-309.
K. Popper (1972) *Objective Knowledge: An Evolutionary Approach* (Oxford: Oxford University Press).
C. Potok (1970) *The Chosen* (Harmondsworth: Penguin).
J. Priestly (1992) 'Response to Brenda Watson' (unpublished paper circulated to participants in 1992 Consultation on 'The Gospel as Public Truth').

C. Raschke (1980) *The Interruption of Eternity: Modern Gnosticism and the Origins of the New Religious Consciousness* (Chicago: Nelson-Hall).
M.B. Reckitt (1935) *Religion and Social Purpose* (London: SPCK).
T. Roszak (1981) *Person/Planet: The Creative Disintegration of Industrial Society* (London: Granada).
—— (1992) *The Voice of the Earth* (New York: Simon & Schuster).
A.L. Rowse (1946) *The Uses of History* (London: Hodder).

L. Sanneh (1989) *Translating the Message: The Missionary Impact on Culture* (Maryknoll, NY: Orbis).
F. Schaeffer (1968) *The God Who Is There* (London: Hodder & Stoughton).
C. Schwöbel (1989) 'Creature of the word: recovering the ecclesiology of the Reformers' in Gunton and Hardy (1989), 110–55.
D. Scott (1985) *Everyman Revived: The Common Sense of Michael Polanyi* (Lewes: The Book Guild).

J. Seabrook (1990) *The Myth of the Market: Promises and Illusions* (Bideford: Green Books).

P. Selby (1991) *BeLonging: Challenge to a Tribal Church* (London: SPCK).

J. Simon and H. Kahn (eds) (1984) *The Resourceful Earth: A Response to Global 2000* (Oxford: Blackwells).

J.W. Sire (1977) *The Universe Next Door: A Guide to World Views* (Leicester: Inter-Varsity Press).

E.C. Stewart (1972) *American Cultural Patterns: A Cross-Cultural Perspective* (Chicago: Intercultural Press).

J.R.W. Stott and R. Coote (eds) (1980) *Down to Earth: Studies in Christianity and Culture* (London: Hodder & Stoughton).

S. Terkel (1975) *Working: People Talk About What They Do All Day and How They Feel About What They Do* (London: Wildwood House).

P. Tillich (1951) *Systematic Theology*, Vol. 1 (London: SCM, 1978).

—— (1964) *Theology of Culture* (New York: Oxford University Press).

—— (1967) *Perspectives on 19th and 20th Century Protestant Theology* (London: SCM).

J.R.R. Tolkien (1954) *The Fellowship of the Ring: Being the First Part of The Lord of the Rings* (London: George Allen & Unwin, 1966).

S. Toulmin (1982) *The Return to Cosmology: Postmodern Science and the Theology of Nature* (Berkeley: University of California Press).

B.J. Walsh (1992) *Subversive Christianity: Imaging God in a Dangerous Time* (Bristol: Regius Press).

S. Weil (1956) *Notebooks* (London: Routledge & Kegan Paul).

S. Weinberg (1977) *The First Three Minutes: A Modern View of the Origin of the Universe* (New York).

L. White Jr (1967) 'The historical roots of our ecologic crisis', *Science*, 155, 1203–07.

B. Williams (1978) *Descartes: The Project of Pure Enquiry* (Harmondsworth: Pelican).

W. Wink (1984) *Naming the Powers: The Language of Power in the New Testament* (Philadelphia: Fortress).

—— (1986) *Unmasking the Powers: The Invisible Forces That Determine Human Existence* (Philadelphia: Fortress).

—— (1992) *Engaging the Powers: Discernment and Resistance in a World of Domination* (Minneapolis: Fortress).

Y. Zamyatin (1972) *We* (Harmondsworth: Penguin).

J. Zizioulas (1985) *Being as Communion: Studies in Personhood and the Church* (London: Darton, Longman & Todd).

Index of Names